THE BDS WAR
AGAINST ISRAEL

THE BDS WAR AGAINST ISRAEL

The Orwellian Campaign
to Destroy Israel
Through the Boycott,
Divestment and Sanctions
Movement

By

JED BABBIN
with HERBERT LONDON

LONDONCENTER
FOR POLICY RESEARCH

The London Center for Policy Research
New York, New York
www.londoncenter.org

Designed by Kristina Phillips

ISBN-13:978-1499606454
ISBN-10:1499606451

Contents

Introduction . . . . *vii*

The BDS War Against Israel . . . . *ix*

Chapter 1

The Ideological and Political Roots of the BDS Movement 11

Chapter 2

Rebutting the Lies 19

Chapter 3

The Durban Strategy, the U.N., and Disinformation 39

Chapter 4

The International BDS Movement 43

Chapter 5

BDS in America 49

Chapter 6

Who Funds the BDS Movement? 55

Chapter 7

Implications for United States and Israeli Policy 63

Epilogue 79

Acknowledgements 83

"A lie repeated a hundred times becomes the truth." —MAO ZEDONG

Introduction

OXFAM AMERICA IS A CHARITABLE ORGANIZATION supported by "global citizens" that aims to end poverty, hunger, and social injustice. It claims to be "one of the most effective international relief and development organizations in the world."

But Oxfam is more than a charity; it is also a propaganda vehicle for the demonization of Israel. Recently Oxfam publicly rebuked one of its own "global goodwill ambassadors," actress Scarlett Johansson. Johansson's offense? Representing SodaStream, an Israeli company in the West Bank. Oxfam suggested it was wrong to promote trade with a company based in "occupied territory." Never mind that the territory is "disputed." One might ignore as well SodaStream's employment of approximately 500 Palestinians; Oxfam knows what is best for the region. To Ms. Johansson's credit, she ended her relationship with the charity, citing "a fundamental difference of opinion in regards to the boycott, divestment and sanctions [BDS] movement."

BDS spokesman Omar Barghouti states the objective of this movement with utter clarity: "The right of Palestinian refugees to return to the homes and lands from which they were displaced and dispossessed in 1948." But there is no such general right. Under one U.N. resolution, Israel was created to be a homeland for the Jewish people. The resolution under which the so-called "right of return" was created was for the Palestinians uprooted by the Israeli war of independence. It didn't encompass the millions of their descendants now living as permanent "refugees" in Jordan, Lebanon, Syria, and other Arab nations. To say otherwise would mean that the U.N. voted to destroy the Jewish homeland one month after it voted to create it. Should the absurd plan of BDS be realized—absurd in the sense that even a great-grandchild of a Palestinian who may live in Jordan, Lebanon, or Syria is considered a refugee—the influx of almost 5 million such "refugees" would cause the state of Israel to cease to exist. Nonetheless, BDS has gained traction, especially in advancing the claim that Israel is a colonial oppressor.

Overlooked in this narrative is the fact that Jewish communities in Iraq, Syria, Iran, Egypt, and Yemen have all been forced out of existence, creating Jewish refugees numbering more than 600,000. The injustices visited on these people are not recognized by the United Nations or even acknowledged by the world media.

While the Middle East is aflame with civil wars, terrorism and anti-humanistic sentiment, Israel has become a major preoccupation in many Western centers of opinion. Yet it is the only democratic, open and truly multiethnic society in the region—the only nation where Jews and Arabs sit side by side in the parliament.

It is instructive that Omar Barghouti, the aforementioned BDS activist, is a graduate of Tel Aviv University. In fact, the university resisted a worldwide petition to have him expelled for his radical views, upholding the principles of academic freedom and free speech, awarding him a master's degree in philosophy. Where in the Muslim world could a story of this kind be told?

In 2014 the valedictorian at Technion University Medical School was a Ms. Mais Ali-Saleh. She is a Muslim who was raised in a small Arab village outside of Nazareth. Most significantly, she is a living example that contradicts BDS claims that Israel is an "apartheid state." Ms. Ali-Saleh noted, "An academic boycott of Israel is a passive move and it doesn't achieve any of its purported objectives." She went on to point out that BDS "perpetrates falsehoods," since Arab women in Israel have more freedom, liberty and academic opportunities than in any Arab country. In fact, she added, Arab countries should be pressured into emulating Israel's academic freedom and democracy.

This viewpoint, however, is submerged before the starry-eyed preaching of Roger Waters, formerly the lead singer of Pink Floyd. In a recent interview, Waters opined that Israel promotes "ethnic cleansing" as part of its "racist apartheid regime," while also drawing parallels to Vichy governments and Nazi Germany. He even described the systematic murder of Jews in the Holocaust as no different from the "murder of Palestinian people." Waters claims many artists share his views, but are fearful of speaking out because of "the powerful Jewish lobby." Of course, Waters's statements actually prove the opposite.

Waters has unlikely allies—well-meaning, often misguided Jews who have accepted the BDS narrative. For many, this is a manifestation of ignorant or unsophisticated opinion; for others, it is the expression of Leftist politics—the latest cause of the professional "do-gooders"; for still others, it is a way to put pressure on the Netanyahu government for greater flexibility in territorial negotiation. Whatever the reasons, BDS has gained considerable ground among American Jews, primarily on college campuses.

There is an important distinction to be drawn between reflexively anti-Zionist radicals such as Norman Finkelstein and Noam Chomsky and "well-meaning" liberal Zionists who believe the BDS movement will actually benefit Israel by accelerating negotiations toward a two-state solution; the New Israel Fund has devoted a significant part of its budget to support BDS. Although the chapters that follow do not emphasize this difference, we are certainly aware of it. However, it is the effect, not the motivation, of various parties that concerns us.

In a recent *Wall Street Journal* op-ed, reporter Lucette Lagnado dissected the BDS movement at her alma mater, Vassar College. A student newspaper piece penned by the president of the Vassar Jewish Union featured all the now-familiar buzzwords: "atrocities," "oppression," "abuse," "colonial," and the always-present "apartheid." Meanwhile, the head of the Jewish Studies program also expressed support for the boycott, demonstrating that the BDS virus has infected academia in seemingly unlikely ways.

Even some Hillels—Jewish college associations—have conceded to the onslaught by encouraging debate on the very existence of Israel, a position in direct violation of the Hillel charter. Under the banner of "a diverse range of opinion," students now openly debate, in a religious Jewish setting, whether Israel should continue to exist. But of course it isn't about open debate and diversity at all; if it were, we'd also see debate and openness on the atrocities occurring daily against Christians in Muslim-dominated countries, and discussion of the differences between the dictates of Sharia and the liberty exercised in Israel.

The bearers of anti-Zionism present their bigotry not as prejudice, but as the pursuit of social justice. Yet the question remains: whose justice? If Zionist thought is the original sin, only dismantling the Jewish state can redress it. Many anti-Zionists claim that they do not oppose Judaism, only the state of Israel. But the main guarantor of Jewish security since the end of World War II has been the sovereign state of Israel. It wasn't born on the ashes of the Holocaust, but it is the last fortress against its reenactment.

Even though the analogy is frequently drawn, BDS is different from the boycott movement that unseated South African apartheid—different in target, different in intent, and different in core morality. Then again, as Chairman Mao maintained, a lie repeated a hundred times becomes the truth. For a generation uneducated about the past, BDS propaganda is like catnip. Its appeal may be irresistible for some, creating a lot of damage in its path. In fact, we are living with some of that damage at the moment.

HERBERT LONDON

THE BDS WAR
AGAINST ISRAEL

THROUGHOUT HISTORY IT HAS BEEN all too common for nations to oppress their peoples by depriving them of basic human rights. France, under The Terror that was part of its 1789 revolution, murdered tens of thousands of civilians, as did the Kaiser's Germany in its march across Belgium in 1914. Nazi Germany committed the Holocaust, Pol Pot's Cambodia tried its hand at genocide, and Stalin's Russia starved and slaughtered millions. The Soviet Union was a model of oppression, sending unnamed tens of thousands to slave labor camps in the Gulag Archipelago described by Solzhenitsyn.

In their time, all of those nations and cultures were outcasts whose only "allies" were conquered militarily, ideologically, or both. Communist China, which massacred millions, has been granted a de facto pardon by the West's turning a blind eye to its 20th-century history, its military buildup and hegemonic ambitions across the Pacific Rim.

Historians were traditionally not shy in reporting that one nation after another fell under the sway of dictators, despots, rogues and terrorists. That continued until after World War II, when the Soviet Union managed to cloak its worst actions because many people around the world fell under its spell of false promises, fraudulent ideology, and mutilated facts. The remnants of that spell continue to benefit some of the world's worst nations, including Putin's neo-Soviet Russia.

In 2014, North Korea continues to murder hundreds of thousands in its version of the Gulag Archipelago. Iran, the world's leading terrorist supporter, may soon be able to extend its hegemony over the entire Middle East because of its nascent nuclear capabilities. Meanwhile, it continues to enjoy a place in the so-called "world community of nations," relieved of sanctions and engaging in diplomacy that is certain to mask its development of nuclear weapons.

Today, several nations—North Korea, Sudan, and Cuba, to name just a few—are rogue nations, penalized for their conduct by economic sanctions and isolation. They exist in a sort of limbo, suspended between the nations that permit basic human rights and those that are tolerant of those nations' ideologies and enslavement of their populations.

Israel has been at war since its birth, its Arab neighbors (except Egypt and Jordan) never having accepted its existence as a nation. It has suffered massive waves of terrorist attacks by Palestinians and groups of terrorists sponsored by nations such as Iran, Syria, and others. Palestinian terrorism has been turned on and off like a faucet, timed to match the tides of the "peace process" that never delivers peace for one principal reason: as we shall see below, the Arab nations have kept the Palestinians in a limbo of their own, the only people in the world who are kept in the permanent status of refugees. They are kept in camps, without any citizenship rights, so that they can be used as a political or terroristic weapon against Israel.[1]

Israel is not a rogue nation or a sponsor of terrorism. It is not ruled by despots or dictators. Its citizens—Jew and Arab alike—equally benefit from the nation's embrace of democracy and human rights. But both within its borders and outside them, a movement of propagandists and disinformationists is working relentlessly to shift world opinion to convince everyone that Israel is as much a rogue nation as is North Korea or Iran. They seek to do this through the so-called "boycott, divestment, and sanctions" movement, or "BDS movement." The movement is propelled by Palestinian activists, Arab governments, and Europeans who join them in their effort to cast Israel out of the global community.

The Palestinians have failed to defeat Israel by terrorism and subversion, so they have settled on the BDS movement as a secondary strategy. As its name implies, "BDS" stands for "boycott, divestment, and sanc-

---

[1] In a 2003 interview with Zia abu Ziad, senior adviser to Yasser Arafat and former Palestinian minister of state, he told Jed Babbin that the Palestinian Authority had stopped terrorist attacks from 1996 to 2000 and resumed them because they didn't gain enough politically. He agreed with the premise that the PA could stop terrorism when it chose to do so (http://old.nationalreview.com/babbin/babbin200311050734.asp).

tions." The movement's stated aims are: (1) to create global boycotts of Israeli universities and industries (purportedly only those that do business in the "occupied" Palestinian territories); (2) to have nations, banks and industries divest themselves of investments in Israeli banks, companies, and the nation as a whole; and (3) to obtain international sanctions against Israel, its economy, and its people.

In the nine years since it formally began, the BDS movement has succeeded to an astonishing degree, finding sympathizers and supporters across the world, but principally in Europe and North America. For most of that time, the Israelis and their government seemed unable to find their voice in opposition to it. Now, however, the BDS movement is finally recognized for what it is: a strategic threat to Israel. As Prime Minister Benjamin Netanyahu said in a March 2014 speech at the AIPAC Policy Conference in Washington, D.C.:

Most people in the BDS movement don't seek a solution of two states for two peoples. On the contrary, they openly admit that they seek the dissolution of the only state for the Jewish people. They're not seeking peace, they're not seeking reconciliation. But some of their gullible fellow travelers actually do believe that BDS advances peace.

Well, the opposite is true. BDS sets back peace because it hardens Palestinian positions and it makes mutual compromise less likely.[2]

Still, the Israelis haven't undertaken a thorough study of the BDS movement—its antecedents, its positions, and its strategy. This book attempts to do that with an urgency of purpose. Because the BDS movement's arguments have been left mostly unanswered, people who are uninformed of the facts and the history that is behind the Israeli-Palestinian conflict risk reaching the wrong conclusion based on sheer inventions. This book is intended to help set the record straight.

The BDS movement's chosen path has been to conduct an amorphous multinational political campaign, much like the antiwar campaigns of the Vietnam era, and as such it has been adopted by the nongovernmental organization (NGO) community, by Palestinian radical activists, and by

---

2 http://www.algemeiner.com/2014/03/04/full-transcript-prime-minister-netanyahu%E2%80%99s-speech-at-2014-aipac-policy-conference/

many in the academic world. Many European governments fund anti-Israel activist NGOs with substantial donations.

The purpose of the BDS movement is to exile Israel to a political ghetto reserved for the world's worst nations. Israel is singled out precisely because it hasn't earned its way into the small club populated by Cuba, Syria, Iran, and North Korea. Because Israel's most serious enemies are themselves Middle Eastern despotisms, they have to convince other nations and people that Israel is as evil and dangerous as they are. Though Israel hasn't earned the status of a pariah, the BDS movement is trying to do that for them. The movement's supporters want to spin enough falsehoods and semitruths to convince people that it is a pariah regardless of the facts.

Though presented in the guise of a humanitarian campaign, the BDS movement is in fact nothing less than an ideological assault on the existence of Israel as a Jewish nation. It is an asymmetrical attack on a nation that seems unprepared or reluctant to engage its enemies in that manner. And, for that reason, it is as great a threat as Israel has ever faced.

The BDS movement has been called the "Third Intifada,"[3] and to understand why, we need to understand the first two. In the aftermath of the 1967 war, in which Israeli forces drove Arab forces across the Jordan River, the U.N. Security Council passed Resolution 242[4], which called for a peace treaty to be negotiated in which Israel would trade lands taken in the war for peace with the Palestinians and its Arab neighbors. In the 20 years between the 1967 war and the First Intifada, there was no progress on any peace deal.

The word "intifada" means "shaking off" in Arabic. The object of the intifadas was to "shake off" Israel from the West Bank area and the strategic Golan Heights that had been seized in the 1967 war. The Israelis believe that to return to the pre-1967 war borders would render the nation vulnerable. The Palestinians demand not only a return to those borders but also a "contiguous" Palestinian state connecting the West Bank and the Gaza Strip. To create a contiguous state for the Palestinians would not be possible without cutting Israel in half.

---

[3] It is called that even by *New York Times* columnist Thomas Friedman. See http://www.nytimes.com/2014/02/05/opinion/friedman-the-third-intifada.html?_r=0.

[4] http://unispal.un.org/U.N.ISPAL.NSF/0/7D35E1F729DF491C85256EE700686136

The First Intifada began in December 1987 when Palestinians attacked Israeli soldiers and civilians with rocks, Molotov cocktails, and hand grenades in protest of the Israeli presence in the West Bank territory.[5] Eventually, a total of about 20,000 people were injured or killed on both sides.[6] Of the fatalities, 1,561 were Palestinians and 421 were Israelis.[7]

The 1993 Oslo Accords seemed to deliver a major step toward peace, because both sides agreed to recognize the other, while the Palestinian Liberation Organization agreed to renounce terrorism and Israel agreed to trade land for peace. None of Israel's Arab neighbors had participated in the negotiations or agreed to those terms.

Peace was enjoyed for the briefest of moments. Though Israel began withdrawing from the West Bank territories, terrorism didn't stop. The suicide bomber became the terrorist weapon of choice for the Palestinians.[8] The Second Intifada, which began on September 29, 2000[9], was fought openly from then on.

Three times since 2000, Israeli prime ministers have tried to implement the "land for peace" theory contained in U.N. Resolution 242. Each time, they offered Palestinian leaders an independent state on far more generous terms than Jordan and Egypt did when they controlled the West Bank and Gaza.[10] In 2000, Israeli Prime Minister Ehud Barak agreed to a plan proposed by President Bill Clinton that would have established a state in the West Bank and Gaza as well as East Jerusalem. But Palestinian Authority President Yasser Arafat walked out of the negotiations and launched the Second Intifada.[11] In 2005, Israeli Prime Minister Ariel Sharon dismantled all Jewish settlements in the Gaza Strip and pulled Israel back across the Israel-Gaza pre-1967 war borders. Within the next two years the Palestinians launched a rain of missiles from Gaza

---

5 http://news.bbc.co.uk/2/hi/329643.stm

6 Id.

7 http://www.btselem.org/statistics/first_intifada_tables

8 http://news.bbc.co.uk/2/hi/middle_east/7381378.stm

9 Id.

10 [full name] Stern, "A Century of Palestinian Rejectionism and Jew Hatred," Encounter Broadsides (2011), p. 39.

11 Id., p. 40.

against Israeli civilians and elected the Hamas terrorist group to govern the Gaza Strip.[12]

In 2008, Prime Minister Ehud Olmert presented Palestinian President Mahmoud Abbas with a detailed map of a proposed Palestinian state composed of almost 100 percent of the West Bank and all of Gaza as well as a formally divided Jerusalem that could have served as the capital of both nations. Olmert's offer was conditioned on the Palestinians conceding the "right of return," which would, if agreed to, create an Arab-Palestinian majority in Israel. Abbas promised to study the map and return for further negotiations. He left with the map and never returned.

By 2001, however, the Palestinians and their Arab sponsors had already decided on a new strategy, one that was incompatible with peace and good-faith negotiations. Though terrorism would continue apace, it would also take a backseat to new methods. This, as we shall see, was the germ of the BDS movement.

Supposedly resulting from a 2005 "call" by "Palestinian civil society," the idea for BDS actually originated in a 2001 meeting held in Tehran, in preparation for the World Conference against Racism, Racial Discrimination, Xenophobia and Related Intolerance later that year in Durban, South Africa. In Tehran, and again in Durban, representatives of Arab nations, Iran, and many countries that had been colonies in the nineteenth and parts of the twentieth centuries met to plot strategies for advancing their grievances against the West. While their stated purpose was to find ways to battle racism, the reality was an orgy of anti-Israeli and anti-American rhetoric.

To justify their campaign for boycotts, divestment, and sanctions, the Palestinians and their allies lodged a host of spurious charges against Israel. The accusations were so absurd and over-the-top that they would have been laughable if they hadn't gained such traction in the global society in the intervening decade.

Here are a few examples, all drawn from the book *Boycott, Divestment and Sanctions,* by the BDS movement's principal writer and spokesman, Palestinian activist Omar Barghouti.

— Israel is "fascist and racist";

— Israel is an "apartheid state";

---

12 Id., pp. 40–41.

— Israel will commit genocide against the Palestinians unless constrained by BDS;

— Israel has committed war crimes against Palestinians in Gaza since 2007;

— Fundamental Jewish religious law provides for massacres and genocide of non-Jewish civilians including children.[13]

In his allegation about Jewish religious law, Barghouti sounds like the writers of the infamous anti-Jewish hoax, *The Protocols of the Elders of Zion*. Although Barghouti's charges amount to nothing more than a collection of lies, distortions, and misinformation, he writes these calumnies as if there were no doubt of their truth. And it is on those very lies that the BDS movement has been built.

Consider this fact: BDS claims that it only wants to end Israel's "occupation" of the West Bank and Gaza Strip. Many of its adherents in Hollywood, the media, and academia have based their support on that single purpose.

But even that announced purpose is a lie, as Barghouti—and many other BDS supporters—have admitted:

> If the occupation ends, let's say, would that end your call for BDS? No, it wouldn't because the Palestinian people are not just suffering from occupation. Yes, Israel's occupation has been going on since 1967 of the West Bank, Gaza, and that includes Jerusalem obviously, but the majority of the Palestinian people are not suffering from occupation only. They are suffering from denial of their right to come back home. The majority of the Palestinians are refugees living in exile and they are denied their right to return to their homes and to their land which is a U.N.-sanctioned right simply because they're non-Jews. Israel, in its own system of apartheid, insists on having a Jewish majority in this land and therefore after ethnically-cleansing the majority of the Palestinians in 1948 to build what is now Israel it refuses to allow them back.[14]

---

13 Barghouti, "Boycott, Divestment and Sanctions," Haymarket Books (2011)

14 https://www.youtube.com/watch?v=qOBg2t6vscc

Some BDS supporters are less skillful than Barghouti in clouding the purpose of the movement. For example:

— As'ad Abu Khalil, a well-known activist in the U.S., wrote, "Justice and freedom for the Palestinians are incompatible with the existence of the state of Israel."[15]

— Ahmed Moor, a pro-BDS author and "Soros fellow,"[16] wrote "Ending the occupation doesn't mean anything if it doesn't mean upending the Jewish state itself."[17]

And some are old-time liberals left over from the Vietnam-era peace movement and their ideological progeny:

— Former Pink Floyd rocker Roger Waters wrote about a letter he sent to Stevie Wonder: "I wrote a letter to him saying that [performing in Israel] would be like playing a police ball in Johannesburg the day after the Sharpeville massacre in 1960. It wouldn't be a great thing to do, particularly as he was meant to be a U.N. ambassador for peace."[18]

— Angela Davis, former communist revolutionary and now Distinguished Professor Emerita at the University of California, Santa Cruz, speaking about a resolution by the American Studies Association to support the BDS movement, said, "The similarities between historical Jim Crow practices and contemporary regimes of segregation in Occupied Palestine make this resolution an ethical imperative for the ASA. If we have learned the most important lesson promulgated by Dr. Martin Luther King—that justice

---

15 http://english.al-akhbar.com/blogs/angry-corner/critique-norman-finkelstein-bds

16 Moor is a fellow of the Paul and Daisy Soros Foundation and received a two-year grant for studies at the Kennedy School of Government (http://www.pdsoros.org/current_fellows/index.cfm/yr/2012#moor).

17 http://mondoweiss.net/2010/04/bds-is-a-long-term-project-with-radically-transformative-potential.html

18 http://www.rollingstone.com/music/news/roger-waters-calls-for-boycott-of-israel-20130320. (In the 1960 Sharpeville massacre, at least 50 black people were murdered by police while protesting peacefully the "pass" laws that restricted black movements in South Africa.

is always indivisible—it should be clear that a mass movement in solidarity with Palestinian freedom is long overdue."[19]

— When the Toronto Film Festival was honoring the 100th anniversary of Tel Aviv, Jane Fonda, Danny Glover, Eve Ensler and other Hollywood liberals signed a letter joining a boycott of the film festival that said, in part, that Tel Aviv was built on violence, ignoring the "suffering of thousands of former residents and descendants."[20]

— Author Alice Walker, an outspoken BDS supporter and participant in the effort of a Turkish ship to break the blockade of the Gaza Strip, said, "[Israeli] settlers are the [Ku Klux] Klan."[21]

Israel has rejected the so-called Palestinian "right of return" because if the "refugees" are allowed back in, where once there were about 760,000 actually displaced people, there are now nearly 5 million descendants who would return to Israel under the Palestinian demand. In a nation of less than 8 million—of whom about 1.3 million are already Arab citizens of Israel—the injection of another 5 million Muslims would turn Israel into an Islamic nation.

This cacophony of falsehood is not answered, debated, or even questioned in Western society at large. Israel's finance ministry even shelved—at least temporarily—a report on the effect of the BDS movement on Israel's economy.[22]

Israel is the only free nation in the Middle East, but its government, its people, and their economic and academic institutions are under an ideological assault by those who would destroy it. Though the campaign is couched in terms of ending the "illegal occupation" of "Palestinian lands," it seeks the destruction of Israel.

---

19 http://www.theasa.net/from_the_editors/item/asa_members_vote_to_endorse_academic_boycott/

20 http://www.israeli-occupation.org/2009-09-05/jane-fonda-joins-boycott-of-toronto-film-festival-over-homage-to-israel/

21 http://cifwatch.com/2012/06/22/antisemitism-with-a-literary-glow-alice-walkers-ugly-caricature-of-israeli-jews/

22 http://www.economist.com/news/middle-east-and-africa/21595948-israels-politicians-sound-rattled-campaign-isolate-their-country

CHAPTER 1

THE IDEOLOGICAL
AND POLITICAL ROOTS
OF THE BDS MOVEMENT

THE BDS MOVEMENT'S IDEOLOGICAL and intellectual roots are found in two historic actions. First, in the Arab League's boycott that has been maintained since 1948, and second, in the Soviet Union's efforts to isolate Israel and condemn Zionism.

According to a 2013 Congressional Research Service (CRS) report, the Arab League—a group of 22 Middle Eastern and African nations— has maintained a boycott of Israeli companies and Israeli-made goods since 1948. As the CRS report describes it:

> The boycott has three tiers. The primary boycott prohibits citizens of an Arab League member from buying from, selling to, or entering into a business contract with either the Israeli government or an Israeli citizen. The secondary boycott extends the primary boycott to any entity world-wide that does business in Israel. A blacklist of global firms that engage in business with Israel is maintained by the Central Boycott Office, and disseminated by Arab League members. The tertiary boycott prohibits an Arab League member and its nationals from doing business with a company that deals with companies that have been blackballed by the Arab League. [23]

Because, as CRS said, the boycott was sporadically applied and only ambiguously enforced, it had an indeterminate effect. That effect was

---

23 https://www.fas.org/sgp/crs/mideast/RL33961.pdf

basically nullified by the 1977 U.S. antiboycott legislation that penalizes any U.S. company that complies with boycotts of Israel.

The Soviet Union's effort to isolate Israel and condemn Zionism began in the mid-1960s, when the Soviets blocked a vote in the United Nations on a resolution to condemn anti-Semitism.[24]

Having thrown their support behind Arab efforts to destroy Israel, the Soviets suffered enormous embarrassment when Israel defeated the Arab states resoundingly in 1967 and in 1973, because Arab forces were largely Soviet-supplied and Soviet-trained. That embarrassment led to the expulsion of Soviet advisers from Egypt in 1973.

Then, in 1974, Yasser Arafat's Palestine Liberation Organization—supposedly separated from Arafat's Fatah terrorist group—was given "observer" status as a national liberation organization in the United Nations.

As these events proceeded, there was an at-first-imperceptible change in how Israel was seen by people around the world. Before the 1967 war and even in its aftermath, Israel was seen as the scrappy underdog, a nation that managed to endure all the terrorism, invasions, boycotts, and everything else the Arab world threw at it. But after 1973 the Arab nations, in conjunction with their Soviet backers, began reversing this perception, tapping into the global propaganda machine the Communist bloc had developed since the time of Stalin. Political groups and nations, especially those with ties to the Soviet bloc, began to paint the Palestinians and the Arabs as the underdogs. Israel was no longer a freedom-loving democracy, but a colonialist oppressor of the innocent Palestinians. Meanwhile, the PLO and other Palestinian groups launched a horrific terror campaign against Israeli civilians, most prominently at the Munich Olympics in 1972.

In August 1975, the Organization of African Unity condemned Israel and South Africa as "racist" and "colonial regimes." It was only because America threatened to leave the United Nations that the U.N. didn't bring Israeli expulsion from the U.N. to a vote.[25]

---

[24] http://jcpa.org/article/the-1975-zionism-is-racism-resolution-the-rise-fall-and-resurgence-of-a-libel/

[25] Id.

The Soviet effort didn't end there. Working in partnership with the PLO, the Soviets drafted a U.N. resolution that condemned Zionism as racism.

Former Romanian General Ion Pacepa, the highest-ranking intelligence officer ever to defect from the KGB, told the story of how this came about. Yasser Arafat—acting on behalf of the Soviets—backed by Castro's Cuba, the Soviet bloc nations, and a coalition of Arab governments, managed to get the "Zionism is racism" resolution to the floor of the General Assembly for debate and a vote with the active help of the Romanian foreign intelligence service.[26] Included in the campaign for the resolution was an effort by the Romanian intelligence service that distributed anti-American and anti-Semitic cartoons clandestinely around the U.N.'s headquarters in New York.

On the occasion of the debate on the resolution, on November 10, 1975, then-U.S. Ambassador to the U.N. Daniel Patrick Moynihan gave perhaps the most memorable speech of his distinguished public career. Moynihan foresaw what would happen as a result of the U.N.'s passing that resolution. Just days before the speech, Nobel laureate and Soviet dissident Andrei Sakharov had said that the U.N. action would give the abomination of anti-Semitism international sanction. Moynihan echoed Sakharov, and went further:

> The abomination of anti-Semitism—as this year's Nobel Peace Laureate Andrei Sakharov observed in Moscow just a few days ago—the abomination of anti-Semitism has been given the appearance of international sanction. The General Assembly today grants symbolic amnesty—and more—to the murderers of the six million European Jews.

Moynihan stated one of the basic truths of Judaism: that it accepts not only those who were born into the religion but anyone—regardless of race, creed or national origin. By that standard, he said:

---

26 Ion Pacepa and Ronald Rychlak, "Disinformation," WND Books (2013), pp. 276–77.

Now I should wish to be understood that I am here making one point, and one point only, which is that whatever else Zionism may be, it is not and cannot be "a form of racism." In logic, the State of Israel could be, or could become, many things, theoretically, including many things undesirable, but it could not be and could not become racism unless it ceased to be Zionist.

Moynihan saw the importance of the U.N.'s actions not only because of the damage done to Israel, but also the damage to the U.N., which had—up to that point—some vestiges of truth in its debates and resolutions. Moynihan continued:

The proposition to be sanctioned by a resolution of the General Assembly of the United Nations is that "Zionism is a form of racism and racial discrimination." Now this is a lie. But as it is a lie which the United Nations has now declared to be a truth, the actual truth must be restated....

The terrible lie that has been told here today will have terrible consequences. Not only will people begin to say, indeed they have already begun to say that the United Nations is a place where lies are told, but far more serious, grave and perhaps irreparable harm will be done to the cause of human rights itself. The harm will arise first because it will strip from racism the precise and abhorrent meaning that it still precariously holds today.

Despite Moynihan's warnings, the resolution passed. The roots of the BDS movement were planted.

Since then, the U.N. has criticized Israel—sometimes harshly—in dozens of resolutions; about four dozen anti-Israel resolutions were vetoed by the United States in the Security Council, the only place where it has a veto. In 2014 alone, there were 21 such resolutions, while only *four* criticized nations other than Israel.[27]

---

[27] http://blog.unwatch.org/index.php/2013/11/25/this-years-22-unga-resolutions-against-israel-4-on-rest-of-world/

Israel has tried to serve as a conscience to the U.N., but it has been consistently ignored. Whether the issue is state-sponsored terrorism in the Arab world, the dangers of Iran's nuclear weapons program, or oppression of women and religious minorities around the globe, Israel's voice is ignored or scorned by the General Assembly. Arab nations, Russia, China and many other totalitarian states have maintained a unified, anti-Israel bloc for four decades.

The Birth of BDS

The BDS movement, as noted above, was the product of a U.N. conference held in Tehran in 2001 and the subsequent World Conference against Racism in Durban, South Africa.

Nongovernmental organizations around the world number in the tens of thousands. Some are legitimate charities and relief organizations. But a very large number are simply vehicles for political action. This was very much in evidence at Durban, supposedly a global conference against racism.

Before the conference began, a preconference meeting of NGOs was held in Tehran. Israeli organizations were deliberately excluded.[28] The principal record of the Tehran conference is a paper written by the late Representative Tom Lantos, a California Democrat, for *The Fletcher Forum of World Affairs*[29] (Lantos was the only Holocaust survivor ever to serve in the U.S. Congress).

According to Lantos's account, the Tehran meeting convened in February 2001 without Israeli delegates or representatives of Israeli nongovernmental organizations because Iran refused to recognize Israel and wouldn't allow visas for any Israeli citizens. Both Australia and New Zealand, two outspoken supporters of Israel, were not allowed to participate. Their bids to gain credentials to the conference were blocked by the Organization of Islamic Conference (OIC), with Malaysia and Pakistan forcing a negative vote.[30] The 57-state OIC is now known as the

---

28 www.ngo-monitor.org/article/ngo_forum_at_durban_conference_

29 Representative Tom Lantos, "The Durban Debacle: An Insider's View of the World Conference Against Racism," The Fletcher Forum, Vol. 26:1 (2002).

30 The 57-state OIC is now known as the Organization of Islamic Cooperation. Among its members is Palestine, which it recognizes as a nation.

Organization of Islamic Cooperation. Among its members is Palestine, which it recognizes as a nation.

At the Tehran meeting, the delegates agreed on a Declaration and Plan of Action, which Lantos quoted as follows:

> The Declaration and Plan of Action agreed to by the delegates in the discriminatory atmosphere of Tehran amounted to what could only be seen as a declaration by the states present of their intention to use the conference as a propaganda weapon attacking Israel. Indeed, the documents not only singled the country out above all others—despite the well-known problems with racism, xenophobia and discrimination that exist all over the world—but also equated its policies in the West Bank with some of the most horrible racist policies of the previous century. Israel, the text stated, engages in "ethnic cleansing of the Arab population of historic Palestine," and is implementing a "new kind of apartheid, a crime against humanity." It also purported to witness an "increase of racist practices of Zionism" and condemned racism "in various parts of the world, as well as the emergence of racist and violent movements based on racist and discriminatory ideas, in particular, the Zionist movement, which is based on race superiority.[31]

In a preparatory meeting in Geneva prior to the Durban conference, the Islamic nations—Egypt, Iran, Iraq, Pakistan, Syria, and the observer from the Palestine Liberation Organization—insisted that the Tehran-crafted language be included and that whenever the Holocaust was referred to, the word be changed to "holocausts" to include the supposed "ethnic cleansing" of Palestinians from Israeli territory. It went even further, with the OIC and PLO delegates insisting that the phrase "anti-Semitism" be connected to the phrase "racist practices of Zionism" and "Zionist practices against Semitism." This, as foreshadowed by the Tehran conference, was the moment the Arab states chose to formalize their disinformation campaign against Israel.

All became ready for the conference in South Africa. Soon after it convened, the U.S. and Israeli delegations walked out in protest, leav-

---

[31] Id., p. 36.

ing the OIC and PLO to do as they pleased. It became an anti-American and anti-Israeli circus.

In a paper published in 2006 by the *Yale Israel Journal*[32], Professor Gerald Steinberg reported on the actions of some 1,250 NGOs in their parallel conference in Durban that completely overshadowed the meetings of government representatives.

According to Steinberg, major actors included Human Rights Watch (HRW), Amnesty International, MIFTA (Hanan Mishrawi's Palestinian activist group), the Palestinian Committee for the Protection of Human Rights and the Environment, and the South African NGO Committee. Steinberg asserts that groups such as these benefit from a "halo effect"— their feel-good names and high-minded rhetoric lead people to presume that they are nothing more than nonpartisan human rights advocates. As a result, they are often afforded great deference in the media and in political circles. Unfortunately, the "halo effect" often masks a radical agenda.

For example, Human Rights Watch Executive Director Kenneth Roth defended the anti-Israel agenda of the conference, telling one interviewer, "Clearly Israeli racist practices are an appropriate topic." When Israeli NGO representatives tried to speak, Reed Brody—HRW's advocacy director—moved to expel them.

As a result of the meeting, the NGO Forum published its "Declaration." The BDS movement's "call" of 2005 appears to be cribbed from it.

The NGO Forum Declaration devotes a whole section to Palestine and the Palestinians:

— Section 419 says that the U.N. should force Israel to allow the "right of return," end the "colonial military occupation" of the West Bank and Gaza Strip, and withdraw from both; calls upon the U.N. to restore the U.N. resolution stating that Zionism is racism; and calls for the U.N. to compel Israel to give up the idea that it is a Jewish state;

— Section 420 calls for the establishment of a war crimes tribunal to investigate Israeli war crimes, genocide, ethnic cleansing, and apartheid in the West Bank and Gaza;

---

32 http://www.ngo-monitor.org/article.php?viewall=yes&id=1958

— Section 421 calls for more awareness and education on Israel's apartheid system and racism;

— Section 422 calls for the creation of a U.N. Special Committee on Apartheid and Other Racist Crimes Against Humanity perpetrated by the Israeli "apartheid regime";

— Section 423 calls for special programs to end media distortions that "dehumanize Palestinians";

— Section 424 calls for an anti-Israeli apartheid movement enforced in the same manner that a movement was supported against South Africa;

— Section 425 calls for "the international community to impose a policy of complete and total isolation of Israel as an apartheid state as in the case of South Africa which means the imposition of mandatory and comprehensive sanctions and embargoes, the full cessation of all links (diplomatic, economic, social, aid, military cooperation and training) between all states and Israel. Call upon the Government of South Africa to take the lead in this policy of isolation, bearing in mind its own historical success in countering the undermining policy of 'constructive engagement' with its own past Apartheid regime";

— Section 426 calls for condemnation of those states that are supporting the "Israeli apartheid state" and "its perpetration of racist crimes against humanity including ethnic cleansing, acts of genocide."[33]

This is the Durban Strategy, which could even more accurately be labeled the "OIC Strategy." All that was left for the authors of the BDS movement to do was change a few words of this "Declaration"—lest they be accused of plagiarizing the Durban NGO Forum product—and send it out as the call of the "Palestinian civil society," a group which is never defined.

---

33 http://i-p-o.org/racism-ngo-decl.htm

CHAPTER 2

REBUTTING THE LIES

THE OBJECT OF IDEOLOGICAL WARFARE is to change peoples' minds. The BDS movement has had almost a 10-year head start on the Israeli defense, which began belatedly in 2013. Regardless of the facts, as Mark Twain once said, "A lie can travel halfway around the world while the truth is still putting on its shoes." It is not as if the Israelis have been complacent, but they make a very damaging assumption: that having witnessed their nation's creation, the fair-minded around the world will remember that event and the subsequent Arab violence and intransigence—and place current events in that context. It was a naïve assumption.

Unfortunately, neither Israel nor America has taken the effort to challenge the lies at the heart of the BDS movement.

There is no need to repeat what Moynihan proved in his great speech of November 1975. His refutation of the charge that Zionism is a racist ideology is conclusive. Zionism is not racism because if it were, it could not be Zionism. As long as Jews accept into their religion anyone from any race, creed, religion or ethnicity—as they have for almost six thousand years—the accusation of racism remains absurd.

But what of the other lies?

The Apartheid Hoax
BDS supporters routinely accuse Israel of being an apartheid nation. This is another example, as we shall see, that turns the plain meaning of a term on its head.

"Apartheid"—which means "apartness" in the Afrikaaner language of South Africa—was the statutory policy of that nation from 1948 to 1989. Under apartheid, racial segregation was mandated, 70 percent of the land was reserved for white use, whites were privileged economically (in eligibility and hiring for jobs), interracial marriage was banned, and the education of blacks was controlled. Opposition to apartheid was banned, and opposition leaders were imprisoned.

About 21 percent of Israel's citizens—roughly 1.7 million people— are Arabs.[34] These are people—and their descendants—who stayed in Israel after the 1948 War of Independence. These people chose, as was their right, Israeli citizenship instead of becoming citizens of the Arab (i.e., Palestinian) state at the time of the partition in accordance with the U.N. resolution.

Israeli Arabs have the right to vote in Israel, just as the U.N. partition resolution provided. (This includes Arab women.) The right to vote was denied black South Africans under apartheid (and the right to vote for women is denied by many Islamic countries). Israeli Arabs can hold elective office, another right denied black South Africans. The Israeli parliament—called the Knesset—has 120 members. There have been Arab members since the first Knesset elections in 1949. Currently, 12 Arabs serve in the parliament.[35]

Arab citizens of Israel are not allowed in the Israeli military because of fears of divided loyalties. The only economic disadvantage is that Arabs are not, then, eligible for the benefits given to members of the Israeli military, though their availability for jobs is greater because their careers are not interrupted by mandatory military service.

One apartheid practice was to control and thus limit the education of blacks in South Africa; there are no such statutes in Israel, and there are many Arab students at Israel's top universities. Meanwhile, schools in Palestinian-controlled territory are well-known hotbeds of anti-Semitic propaganda, and are even used for more nefarious purposes, such as a November 2007 rocket attack launched from a Palestinian school in the Gaza Strip.[36]

South African Judge Richard Goldstone led a U.N. Human Rights Commission to investigate allegations of war crimes committed by Israelis

---

34 http://www.jewishvirtuallibrary.org/jsource/Society_&_Culture/arabstat.html

35 https://www.jewishvirtuallibrary.org/jsource/Politics/knesset.html

36 http://www.un.org/apps/news/story.asp?NewsID=24593&Cr=palestin&Cr1=

in the Gaza conflict of 2008–2009, discussed below. In a *New York Times* op-ed that appeared on October 31, 2011, Goldstone wrote:

> In Israel, there is no apartheid. Nothing there comes close to the definition of apartheid under the 1998 Rome Statute: "Inhumane acts ... committed in the context of an institutionalized regime of systematic oppression and domination by one racial group over any other racial group or groups and committed with the intention of maintaining that regime." Israeli Arabs—20 percent of Israel's population—vote, have political parties and representatives in the Knesset and occupy positions of acclaim, including on its Supreme Court. Arab patients lie alongside Jewish patients in Israeli hospitals, receiving identical treatment.[37]

To say that Israel is an "apartheid" country is not only a lie, but a clumsy one. The facts are so clear that any examination of them immediately reveals the falsehood.

War Crimes and Genocide

Israel's 2006 campaign in Lebanon was precipitated by Lebanese Hizballah terrorists who raided Israel and kidnapped two Israeli soldiers. They did so in coordination with the Hamas terrorists that, since that same year, have governed the Gaza Strip.[38]

This action is just one source of the accusations of "war crimes." That charge is repeated casually, usually in respect to Israeli military strikes on terrorists in the Gaza Strip. Barghouti took it further, claiming that only the destruction of Israel's economy will stop a Palestinian genocide. In combination they make a calumny so vile that it could only be repeated by those willfully ignorant of the facts.

In the heavy fighting in Lebanon in 2006, Hizballah famously practiced "fauxtography"—it Photoshopped and staged photos of supposed war crimes.[39] Hizballah fighters and sympathetic media invented war-

---

37   http://www.nytimes.com/2011/11/01/opinion/israel-and-the-apartheid-slander.html

38   http://www.nytimes.com/2006/07/14/opinion/14young.html

39   http://littlegreenfootballs.com/

crime stories that were picked up all over the world, such as pictures that purportedly showed Israel intentionally targeting ambulances.[40] Terrorists dug up or moved dead bodies—including those of women and children—to places the Israelis had struck to manufacture "evidence" of war crimes.[41] Some news outlets ran photographs that had been altered to make the attacks seem more severe than they were.[42] Reuters, for example, withdrew one photograph after finding it had been altered.[43]

This Palestinian "fauxtography" was only part of the disinformation campaign that accompanied the action in Lebanon. From December 2008 to January 2009, the Israeli military conducted "Operation Cast Lead," in which Israel struck the terrorist forces of Hamas in the Gaza Strip. It began with the targeted killing of Hamas military commander Ahmed al-Jaabari.[44]

Since 1997, Hamas has been designated a foreign terrorist group by the State Department. Nonetheless, in 2006 the Palestinians elected Hamas to be the government of the Gaza Strip by a large majority.[45]

Hamas is dedicated to Israel's destruction. Its charter document says, in part, "The purpose of HAMAS is to create an Islamic Palestinian state throughout Israel by eliminating the State of Israel through violent jihad."[46] Everything, then, coming from the Hamas government, Hamas members, and sympathizers (i.e., the majority of Palestinians who chose Hamas to govern Gaza)—which means virtually everything coming out of the Gaza Strip—has to be regarded as propaganda and misinformation unless and until proven true. It cannot be relied on to state any truth about Israel.

Nevertheless, the allegations of war crimes coming out of "Operation Cast Lead" were so intense that a special U.N. Human Rights

---

[40] http://www.zombietime.com/fraud/ambulance/

[41] http://littlegreenfootballs.com/article/22071_Photographer_Alleges_Unearthing_of_Bodies

[42] Id. at note 45. See also http://www.ynetnews.com/articles/0,7340,L-3286966,00.html.

[43] http://www.ynetnews.com/articles/0,7340,L-3286966,00.html

[44] http://www.foreignpolicy.com/articles/2012/11/14/operation_cast_lead_20

[45] http://www.washingtonpost.com/wp-dyn/content/article/2006/01/26/AR2006012600372.html

[46] Andrew McCarthy, "The Grand Jihad," Encounter Books (2010), p. 136.

Council (UNHRC) mission, under South African Judge Richard Goldstone, was appointed to investigate them. Because the UNHRC has had a long record of criticizing Israel, the Israelis refused to cooperate. In its initial report, the Goldstone investigation accused Israel of targeting civilians intentionally, and said—correctly—that the Hamas terrorists had also been targeting Israeli civilians.[47]

Israelis were outraged, and commenced their own investigations. As a result of these and other investigations subsequent to his, Judge Goldstone ultimately retracted a significant part of his original report. In an April 1, 2011, *Washington Post* op-ed, Goldstone admitted that Israel had not intentionally targeted civilians as a matter of policy (though he didn't exonerate individual soldiers). He also reaffirmed that Hamas had clearly and deliberately committed war crimes. Goldstone added, "That the crimes allegedly committed by Hamas were intentional goes without saying—its rockets were purposefully and indiscriminately aimed at civilian targets." [48]

Also significant, Goldstone wrote, was that while Israel had conducted numerous investigations into these alleged war crimes, Hamas hadn't conducted any. The inescapable conclusion is that the commission of war crimes was Hamas policy and its leadership was content to rest on that record.

In November 2012, during the fighting between Israeli forces and Palestinian terrorists in the Gaza Strip, about 1,500 rockets were fired into Israel, aimed at civilian population centers.[49] Even the Human Rights Watch group, which had demonstrated its general anti-Israeli ideology in the Durban Conference in 2001, condemned these attacks as war crimes.

Have there been civilian casualties in Lebanon, Gaza, and other places where Israel has attacked Palestinian terrorists? Of course there have. They are regrettable tragedies, as were the ambulances hit by Israel aircraft in 2006. They are not, however, war crimes.

---

47 http://www.washingtonpost.com/wp-dyn/content/article/2009/09/15/
AR2009091503499.html

48 http://www.washingtonpost.com/opinions/reconsidering-the-goldstone-report-on-israel-and-war-crimes/2011/04/01/AFgl11JC_story.html

49 http://www.haaretz.com/news/diplomacy-defense/human-rights-watch-palestinians-committed-war-crimes-during-gaza-war.premium-1.489649

About genocide, it is necessary to say more than the obvious, i.e. that genocide is anathema to the members of a religion that suffered the Holocaust. Anyone who has visited the Yad Vashem Holocaust museum in Jerusalem has seen some of the dozens of Jewish children who visit every day; it implants the lessons of the Holocaust in a way that makes it unthinkable for Jews to commit similar brutalities. And it is for that very reason that Israel is being accused of that crime by BDS proponents.

For example, Barghouti's book, citing allegations in a paper by the Al Dameer Association for Human Rights in Gaza, alleges that Israel chose to use toxic weapons in the Gaza incursion that caused a dramatic increase in cancer, birth defects, and miscarriages. He writes:

> The above, mostly ongoing, Israeli crimes do not occur in a vacuum; they are products of a culture of impunity, racism and genocidal tendencies that has overtaken Israeli society shaping its mainstream discourse and "commonsense" approach to the "Palestinian problem."[50]

He goes on to write that the war crimes consist of ordering soldiers to indiscriminately shoot civilians in residential buildings and civilian neighborhoods.[51] As shown below, in his recanting of many of the allegations in the Goldstone report, Judge Goldstone found that Israel had no policy of intentionally killing civilians and that regarding the instances of such crimes occurring, they were investigated by the proper Israeli authorities.[52]

The 1948 International Convention on the Prevention and Punishment of Genocide defines it as any of the following acts committed with intent to destroy, in whole or in part, a national, ethnical, racial, or religious group, as such: (a) killing members of the group; (b) causing serious bodily or mental harm to members of the group; (c) deliberately inflicting on the group conditions of life calculated to bring about its physical destruction in whole or in part; (d) imposing

---

[50] Supra, Barghouti, p. 40

[51] Supra, note 41

[52] http://www.washingtonpost.com/opinions/reconsidering-the-goldstone-report-on-israel-and-war-crimes/2011/04/01/AFgl11

measures intended to prevent births within the group; or (e) forcibly transferring children of the group to another group.[53]

None of the accusations of genocide against Israel cite one shred of evidence.[54] Never have Israeli policies or actions had the intent of destroying the Palestinians as a group, in whole or in part. For BDS leaders to say otherwise is perhaps their most monstrous lie.

The Gaza Blockade and the Walls

In May 2010, Israeli forces stopped the Turkish ship *Mavi Marmara* in international waters. The ship was planning in a very publicized way to run the Israeli blockade on the Gaza Strip, ostensibly to deliver humanitarian supplies.[55]

When the Israelis boarded the ship, they were reportedly attacked by passengers and crew members. As a result, nine people were killed. The Turkish government protested, and recriminations against Israel went round the world very quickly.

U.N. Secretary General Ban Ki-Moon appointed a four-man panel under British Sir Jeffrey Palmer to investigate. The Palmer investigation made three crucial findings. First, it said that when the Israelis boarded the vessel, they were met with organized violence and had to defend themselves. Second, the report found that Israel faces "a real threat to its security from military groups in Gaza"; and third, in recognition of that threat, "The naval blockade was imposed as a legitimate security measure in order to prevent weapons from entering Gaza by sea and its implementation complied with the requirements of international law."[56]

In short, the Gaza sea blockade is legal under international law.

So is the fence that surrounds the Gaza Strip. And so is the fence around the West Bank.

From the beginning of the Second Intifada—about September 2000—until the first continuous section of the Gaza wall was built in

---

53 http://www.icrc.org/applic/ihl/ihl.nsf/ART/357-02?OpenDocument

54 http://www.mfa.gov.il/MFA/MFA-Archive/2000/Pages/Terrorism%20deaths%20in%20Israel%20-%201920-1999.aspx

55 http://www.cnn.com/2010/WORLD/meast/05/31/gaza.protest/

56 http://www.nytimes.com/2011/09/02/world/middleeast/02flotilla.html?pagewanted=all&_r=0

July 2003, about 73 terrorist attacks emanated from Gaza, killing about 293 Israelis and wounding another 1,950.[57] Between August 2003 and June 2004, only three attacks were successful, and they all occurred in the first half of 2003.[58] When Jed Babbin visited Israel in late 2003, Israeli officials told him that the number of attacks emanating from Gaza had dropped to zero.

In 2004, the International Court of Justice (ICJ) ruled that it was illegal under international law for the Israelis to construct a barrier fence along the West Bank.[59] The ICJ reasoned that it was a de facto annexation of Palestinian land and thus not allowed under the U.N. Charter.

That the court, which is an agency of the United Nations, got many things wrong is not surprising. At any given time, several of its "judges" are from nations whose governments are the very ones who have made up the anti-Israel bloc since the 1970s. At this writing, judges from Morocco, Somalia, and Uganda—nations not known for protecting their citizens' human rights or for their law-abiding judiciaries—are among the 15 sitting judges.[60]

The ICJ simply ignored the clause of the U.N. Charter that overrides all the others. Article 51 of Chapter VII says, in part, "Nothing in the present Charter shall impair the inherent right of individual or collective self-defense if an armed attack occurs against a Member of the United Nations, until the Security Council has taken measures necessary to maintain international peace and security."[61]

What this means is that Israel's right to self-defense, in the continued absence of U.N. Security Council action to defend it against the threats that emanate from the other side of the barriers, makes both fences—the one around the Gaza Strip and the one along the West Bank—legal under international law. As long as the Palestinians use terrorism emanating from Gaza and the West Bank as weapons, as long as they refuse to recognize Israel as a Jewish state, those walls and fences are necessary to the security of Israeli citizens. Regardless, since the court's ruling, the

---

[57] https://www.jewishvirtuallibrary.org/jsource/Peace/fence.html

[58] https://www.jewishvirtuallibrary.org/jsource/Peace/fence.html

[59] http://www.icj-cij.org/docket/files/131/1671.pdf

[60] http://www.icj-cij.org/court/index.php?p1=1&p2=2&p3=1

[61] http://www.un.org/en/documents/charter/chapter7.shtml

Israeli government has changed the route of the barrier to eliminate most of the intrusions into the West Bank to which the court objected.[62]

Another part of the objections to the barrier says that Article 51 can only be invoked in respect to actions of nations. That is a misreading of the plain language of Article 51, which does not limit its applicability to attacks by one nation against another. Moreover, the Palestinians insist they are a nation and the U.N. has granted them nonmember pseudo-national status. They cannot have it both ways.

The ICJ's singling out of Israel's terrorist barriers is telling. Professor Michael Curtis explains that fences and walls are commonplace all over the world—used to separate warring peoples from the time the Great Wall of China was built, to Hadrian's Wall, to the DMZ between the two Koreas.[63] Curtis writes:

> Barriers are very common. They exist throughout the world, in every continent, for a variety of reasons. Some, as in the Soviet Union and Communist countries and especially the Berlin Wall from 1961 to 1989, are created to prevent citizens from leaving a territory. Many others exist to prevent people from entering a territory—either a country or a particular area within it. Some have been established to separate parties involved in a conflict or to prevent the conflict altogether, as in Belfast in 1969 and in Londonderry; Cyprus in 1974; Kuwait-Iraq in 1991; Kashmir in 2004; and the two Koreas in 1953. Some have been set up to prevent undesirable activity, as in India to stop drug-smuggling and terrorism from Burma, or on the Kazakh-Uzbekistan border.

He adds:

> Barriers against terrorism are also common. The more important ones are those built by Russia against Chechnya, Pakistan against Afghanistan, Malaysia against Thailand, India against Burma, and Egypt against Gaza in 1979.

---

62 http://www.tufi.org.uk/israeli_palestinian_conflict/security-barrier-briefing.html
63 http://www.americanthinker.com/2011/08/a_fence_for_defense.html

The ICJ's condemnation of the barrier around the West Bank without a word or decision on other similar walls delivers the final blow to the court's credibility.

Barghouti's Blood Libel 2.0

Barghouti's incitement of hatred for Jews echoes the anti-Semitic blood libel of czarist Russia's "Protocols of the Elders of Zion." He writes:

> It is crucial to note that fundamentalist interpretation of the Halacha, or Jewish law, openly justify massacres, even genocide (as in mass murder of "non-Jewish" civilians, including children) in what is termed a "war of revenge" or "necessary war." A war of necessity in fundamentalist teachings would be waged against the entire "enemy" population without sparing anyone. The only limit is on committing any act that might lead to more injury of the Jewish community in retribution. So if a massacre of, say, ten thousand Gentiles would cause damage to Israel that outweighed the "benefits," it should be avoided. This is the sole consideration that is allowed in such fanatical religious teachings, which have become dominant among the religious Zionist community in Israel and beyond and have seeped into the thinking of the general Israeli public in many ways.[64]

Barghouti's only citation for this calumny is an article he wrote himself. Rabbi Binyamin Sendler is a noted Talmudic scholar and an expert on Jewish religious law. He investigated the claims made in Barghouti's book and found them entirely false:

> To say that Jewish religious law allows or even encourages mass murder of non-Jews (including children) is completely false. The Talmud divides the Gentile nations between the idolators (the "Akum") and the godly Gentiles (the "Ger Toshav"). The idol worshippers are viewed with great suspicion. To murder an Akum is obviously

---

[64] Supra, Barghouti, pp. 42–43.

prohibited. (See Tractate Avodah Zarah 13b, Maimonides; laws of murder 4:11, 2:11.) The godly Ger Toshav are required to be treated equally with Jews.

There is one exception to the Halacha, regarding the Amalekites, a people who G-d labeled as the embodiment of evil and upon whom unlimited war was sanctioned. However, the cogent point regarding this exception is that there is no country, group of people, or single person alive today who is identified in any way as an Amalekite. This fact is testified to by every reputable Halachic source.

There is some BDS-related writing that tries to say that Muslims or other kinds of Gentiles are within the "Amalek" exception to the bar against murder. Rabbi Sendler debunked that conclusively:

> I understand that some of the references you have found quote a chapter by Isaac Shahak in which he cited a responsa by the Chatam Sofer who equated certain gentiles with Amalek. It was absolutely inconceivable to me that the revered Chatam Sofer would write such an utter absurdity. It required quite a bit of investigation for me to discover the responsum referred to (its number was mis-cited, and there are four volumes of responsa). However, when I did find it, I discovered that this portion of the responsa was fabricated out of whole cloth, and the Chatam Sofer make no such claim or inference.

Regardless of Mao's statement that a lie repeated a hundred times becomes the truth, this lie remains a lie no matter how many times Barghouti and the BDS supporters repeat it.

Barghouti's admission that the BDS movement demands that all of the five million "Palestinian refugees" in other nations be given the "right of return" to Israel means that Israel would be made into an Islamic state by their emigration. And for Israel to become an Islamic state would turn it into a nation like Saudi Arabia, Iraq, Iran, and so many other Islamic nations that deny basic human rights to their citizens.

If you support the BDS movement, you are also supporting the lies at the root of its arguments. Similarly, you are not supporting Palestinian rights, you are de facto working for the delegitimization and destruction of Israel.

Ethnic Cleansing?

As previously discussed, approximately 700,000 Arab Palestinians emigrated from the Jewish state when it was partitioned by the U.N. in 1948. The mass emigration began in 1947, before partition of the British Mandate, and continued through the Israeli War of Independence in 1948–1949.

In 1917, dividing up much of the territory of what had been the Ottoman Empire, France and England (under the aegis of the League of Nations) imposed the British Mandate in Palestine. It encompassed all the land that is now Israel, the Gaza Strip, and the area east of the Jordan River that is now the Kingdom of Jordan. (France became the ruler of the areas that are now Syria and Lebanon.)

In that same year, the Balfour Declaration, named after Britain's Foreign Minister, declared British support for the establishment of a Jewish homeland in Palestine and promised to safeguard the civil and religious rights of the Arab inhabitants.

In 1919, Prince Faisal—who led, with T.E. Lawrence, the Arab revolt against the Turks in World War I—signed a declaration with Zionist leader Chaim Weitzman that said that "all necessary measures should be taken to encourage and stimulate immigration of Jews into Palestine on a large scale."[65] Faisal, later the King of Jordan, changed his mind and demanded that Britain reserve Palestine for Arabs. Jews were subsequently forbidden to settle in 80 percent of the British Mandate territory.

Since Roman times, Jews had always been a minority in Palestine. When Zionists began emigrating in large numbers after the Balfour Declaration, any hope of peace between Jews and Arabs quickly evaporated. Riots and pogroms in 1920 and 1929 took many Jewish lives. The growing hatred of Jewish settlers among Palestinian Arabs led to a 1936 general strike. In 1937, the British Peel Commission recommended partition

---

[65] Supra, Stern, p. 8

of the Mandate into Jewish and Arab states. The Jews were divided, but the Arab Higher Committee—a group of tribal leaders and wealthy Arabs—opposed the Peel plan, and the British abandoned the idea.

Palestinian Arab society in 1947 was generally split between farm villages and the third of Arabs who lived in towns and cities.[66] The towns and cities had been stagnant for centuries. Members of several dozen elite families were recognized as leaders, but there was no organized government, nationalism, or idea of statehood.

The most important political figure was the Mufti of Jerusalem, Amin al-Husseini, who has been called the father of Palestinian radicalism. He lived in Berlin from 1941 to 1945 and was closely identified with the Nazi regime, including Hitler. In 1941, addressing Husseini directly, Hitler said:

> Germany stands for an uncompromising struggle against the Jews. It is self-evident that the struggle against the Jewish national homeland in Palestine forms part of this struggle, since such a national homeland would be nothing other than a political base for the destructive influence of Jewish interests. Germany also knows that the claim that Jewry plays the role of an economic pioneer in Palestine is a lie. Only the Arabs work there, not the Jews. Germany is determined to call on the European nations one by one to solve the Jewish problem and, at the proper moment, to address the same appeal to non-European peoples.[67]

In 1947 Palestine, there were between 1.2 and 1.3 million Arabs, including about 150,000 Christians. Most of the land was farmed, and about half of the farmland was owned by large absentee landholders in Egypt, Syria and Jordan. By the end of 1947, there were 1.9 million people living in the Mandate area, 31 percent of whom were Jewish.[68]

---

66 Benny Morris, "The Birth of the Palestinian Refugee Problem 1947–1949," pp. 9–11

67 In 1943, the Nazis considered exchanging 5,000 Jewish children for captured German soldiers. The Mufti lobbied Himmler against the release, and the children were sent to the death camps. See "Stern, A Century of Palestinian Rejectionism and Jew Hatred," pp. 28–29.

68 http://www.thejerusalemfund.org/ht/d/ContentDetails/i/2963

In November 1947, the U.N. passed General Assembly Resolution 181, which created a Jewish state in what was to be—until May 1948—the British Mandate in Palestine. Under the resolution, both Arabs and Jews could opt for citizenship either in Jewish Israel or in the declared Arab areas outside it, with the right to vote in either land of their choice.[69]

If the non-Jewish citizens of the new state of Israel had accepted the terms of Resolution 181, there would never have been "Palestinian" refugees from Israel.

The Arab Higher Committee, led by Mufti Husseini, rejected partition and immediately launched a wave of terrorist attacks on Jews, which quickly evolved into Arab militias clashing with Israeli forces.

According to historian Benny Morris, the Arab exodus from the British Mandate lands came in waves: the first, from December 1947 to March 1948, and the second, from April to June 1948. The others occurred during the Israeli War of Independence (May 1948 to June 1949).[70]

The first wave occurred in the confusion that resulted from the approach of the British withdrawal (scheduled for August 1948). It was a time in which Arab militias and Jewish forces fought a combined guerilla and conventional war.[71] Much of the confusion was the result of Arab leaders who were alternately demanding that the Arab-Palestinians stay put and that they go to Arab lands.

In May 1948, *Time* magazine reported, "The mass evacuation, prompted partly by fear, partly by orders of Arab leaders, left the Arab quarter of Haifa a ghost city.... By withdrawing Arab workers their leaders hoped to paralyze Haifa." Similarly, in October 1948, *The Economist* reported, "Of the 62,000 Arabs who formerly lived in Haifa not more than 5,000 or 6,000 remained. Various factors influenced their decision to seek safety in flight. There is but little doubt that the most potent of the factors were the announcements made over the air by the Higher Arab Executive, urging the Arabs to quit.... It was clearly intimated that those

---

69 http://www.yale.edu/lawweb/avalon/un/res181.htm

70 Supra, Morris, pp. 29–131

71 Id., pp. 30-31

Arabs who remained in Haifa and accepted Jewish protection would be regarded as renegades."[72]

As Khaled Al-Azm, Syria's Prime Minister, said after the 1948 war:

Since 1948 it is we who demanded the return of the refugees ... while it is we who made them leave.... We brought disaster upon ... Arab refugees, by inviting them and bringing pressure to bear upon them to leave.... We have rendered them dispossessed.... We have accustomed them to begging.... We have participated in lowering their moral and social level.... Then we exploited them in executing crimes of murder, arson, and throwing bombs upon ... men, women and children—all this in the service of political purposes.[73]

The Arab militias were under the command of Mufti Husseini; despite that, there were a number of local peace treaties negotiated between the Jews and individual Arab villages. There was a relative peace during the first months of 1948 that allowed the harvesting of the citrus crop. In February to March 1948, about 75,000 Arabs from cities such as Haifa, Jerusalem, and Jaffa moved east. Many more followed from the Coastal Plain area and farm villages after they had been attacked by one side or the other or simply in fear of attack.

The second wave occurred in an increasingly confused and violent time. The British evacuation was, by June, imminent. Jewish forces in Jerusalem were besieged; the roads were the common site of attacks on Jewish supply convoys; during April and May, dozens of Arab villages were abandoned. Massive numbers of people fled the fighting.

On May 14, 1948, Israel declared its independence. In its proclamation, Israel said, "We appeal—in the very midst of the onslaught launched against us now for months—to the Arab inhabitants of the State of Israel to preserve peace and participate in the upbuilding [sic] of the State on the basis of full and equal citizenship and due representation in all its provisional and permanent institutions." The Arab nations began their war against Israel the following day. Armies from Lebanon, Syria, Iraq,

---

72 http://www.jewishfederations.org/page.aspx?id=121275

73 http://www.eretzyisroel.org/~jkatz/refugees2.html

and Egypt attacked. (Saudi Arabia sent a unit that fought under Egyptian command.)[74]

Even before the war began, Israel was pressured to allow the Arabs to return to the Palestinian area. The leader of that effort was Count Folke Bernadotte, the United Nations mediator appointed to oversee the transition from the British Mandate to the partitioned new states. The Jewish government decided that the return of the Palestinians before war's end would be too great a risk. David Ben-Gurion, Israel's first Prime Minister, became entrenched in the rejection of any return so long as any invading army was on Israeli soil.

When the war was over, there was a stalemate. In passing Resolution 194—the one Barghouti says provides a "right of return"—it was understood by Israel, Bernadotte, and by the U.N. powers that the bulk of the refugees would not be repatriated under that authority. It could not have been misunderstood by the Palestinians.

The war over partition was a war over land claimed under international law—both the British Mandate and the U.N. resolution on partition—by the Jewish people that the Arabs in Palestine and the surrounding Arab nations sought to deny. As happens in almost every war, people fled their homes in fear of being caught in the fighting. Many others were driven out. Some stayed and were hurt or killed. There were towns and villages destroyed or abandoned, while others were left untouched. But it was not an ethnic cleansing.

Compare the war and exodus of refugees with real ethnic cleansing, as exemplified by Serbian leaders Ratko Mladic and Radovan Karadzic and their reign of terror in Bosnia.

Mladic has been tried in Geneva for the 1995 massacre of about 7,000 Muslims in the town of Srebrenica and other war crimes. Remains are still being buried in Srebrenica. [75]

Thirty-eight of Mladic's fellow Serbs have already been convicted of war crimes including genocide in their effort to rid their nation of Muslims. Serbian leader Karadzic is also being tried for those crimes.

---

[74] http://history.state.gov/milestones/1945-1952/arab-israeli-war

[75] http://www.foxnews.com/world/2013/07/11/bosnia-to-bury-hundreds-at-srebrenica-massacre-site/

The differences between Mladic's and Karadzic's vicious crimes and what happened to the Arabs during the last year of the British Mandate and Israel's War of Independence are obvious to any unbiased observer. In "ethnic cleansing," civilians are intentionally targeted for massacre and forced expulsion.

That is a point that cannot be emphasized too greatly. The Geneva Conventions of 1949 make it clear that in war, military forces have no right to intentionally harm civilians.

There were no Srebrenica-like massacres in Israel's war to defeat the Palestinian militias and the Arab armies, both of which were conducting their own campaigns to eliminate Jews from Palestine. Though the Jews certainly bear some responsibility for the number of Palestinians who fled before and during the war, so do the Arab leaders who told them they had to leave. Indeed, it is almost certain that if victorious, the Arab armies would have inflicted genocide and ethnic cleansing on the hundreds of thousands of Jewish civilians.

On the day after Israel declared its independence and the five Arab armies invaded, the Arab League published a statement in which they again rejected partition and said that they intended to force creation of a unitary Palestinian state.[76] They meant to destroy Israel by force of arms. There is no reason to believe they would have treated defeated Jews any differently from the way Mladic treated Bosnian Muslims.

In the more than six decades since Israel's founding, the Arab nations have made it very clear that they do not want to solve the Palestinian refugee issue. Egypt has refused Palestinians entry since the 1948 war, while both Syria and Lebanon denied Palestinians the right to settle there. Only Jordan allowed Palestinians to become citizens, and it claimed what is now the West Bank territory in the process.[77]

Today's principal population of Palestinians is not in the West Bank or Gaza. Rather, they are imprisoned in refugee in camps in Jordan (341,000), Lebanon (226,500), and Syria (127,800), while more than double that number live in those nations outside the camps.[78]

---

76 http://www.mideastweb.org/arableague1948.htm

77 http://www.jewishfederations.org/page.aspx?id=47015

78 http://prrn.mcgill.ca/background/index.htm

The Palestinian refugees have a special U.N. organization dedicated to their welfare, the United Nations Relief and Works Agency for Palestine Refugees in the Near East (UNRWA). In 1958, UNRWA's Ralph Galloway declared while in Jordan that:

> The Arab states do not want to solve the refugee problem. They want to keep it as an open sore, as an affront to the United Nations, and as a weapon against Israel. Arab leaders do not give a damn whether Arab refugees live or die.[79]

It is precisely as Khaled Al-Azm said after the 1948 war: the Arab nations have no regard for the lives or fortunes of the Palestinians. They are far more interested in maintaining the Palestinians as a useful weapon against Israel than in helping the Palestinians economically, socially, or in any other way. Arab nations have been notably absent from the "peace process" between the Israelis and Palestinians, engineered at times by the U.S. They were not at the negotiating table in 2000, 2005, or 2008. They have not been at the table in the 2014 round propelled by President Barack Obama and Secretary of State John Kerry.

Instead of joining in and encouraging a peace between Israel and the Palestinians, the Arab nations stand aloof, only pressuring the United States to demand more concessions from the Israelis. They exert control over the negotiations, but only to prevent agreement. As a recent example, before the Abbas-Obama meeting in March 2014, State Department spokeswoman Jen Psaki told the Palestinian newspaper *Al-Quds* that it was not necessary for Palestinians to recognize Israel as a Jewish state.[80] Seizing on this apparent change in American policy, the Arab League foreign ministers immediately replied en masse that Palestinians would never do so.[81]

---

[79] http://www.eretzyisroel.org/~jkatz/refugees2.html#18

[80] http://www.breitbart.com/Big-Peace/2014/03/09/State-Dept-Palestinians-Do-Not-Need-to-Recognize-Israel-as-Jewish-State

[81] http://www.foxnews.com/world/2014/03/09/arab-league-chief-calls-on-arabs-to-take-firm-stand-against-recognizing-israel/

No "Right of Return"

The "right of return" is the notion that every Arab person who chose to leave the Jewish state at the time the U.N. divided the area of the British mandate in 1948—as well as any of their children, grandchildren, and anyone else the United Nations chooses to call a Palestinian "refugee"— have the right to emigrate to Israel and become citizens. This so-called "right" is, like the "fauxtography" in Lebanon, invented.

Begin with the terms of U.N. Resolution 181, dated November 29, 1947. This is the partition plan that created an Arab state and a Jewish state. (The term "Jewish state" is used repeatedly throughout the resolution.) Each is to be self-governing, with citizens of either—before the Mandate expired—enabled to move to the other.

Though some U.N. members may wish it were not so, Resolution 181 created a Jewish state. Which means that the Jewish people would, then and now, be self-governing.

At the time of the partition, about 600,000 to 726,000 Palestinian Arabs moved voluntarily or involuntarily from the territory that became Israel.[82] A later U.N. resolution, 184 (December 11, 1948), says that "refugees wishing to return to their homes and live at peace with their neighbors should be permitted to do so at the earliest practicable date, and that compensation should be paid for the property of those choosing not to return and for loss of or damage to property which, under principles of international law or in equity, should be made good by the Governments or authorities responsible."

The BDS movement translates that into a "right" to return, which they assert Israel is compelled by international law to obey.

Israel's current population is a bit over 8 million, of which 6.1 million are Jews and 2.5 million are non-Jews. In the latest population figures available, there are almost 4.7 million Palestinian "refugees" in five Arab states.

If you allow the immigration of 4.7 million Palestinian "refugees," the Jewish population in Israel would become a large minority, and the idea of a "Jewish state" would disappear, because the Jewish minority could not be self-governing. Resolution 184 was written to encourage

---

[82] Morris, supra, pp. 297–98.

the return of only the original Palestinian refugees, not to destroy the idea of a Jewish-governed state that the U.N. had created only two weeks earlier. Adding the future generations that the 4.7 million Palestinians comprise would immediately and completely prevent Jewish self-government, which was the point of U.N. Resolution 181.

Whether apartheid, war crimes, racism, or any of the other charges with which the BDS movement tries to delegitimize Israel, they are all manifestly false. Why, then, is the BDS movement able to get so many people to agree with them?

CHAPTER 3

THE DURBAN STRATEGY, THE U.N., AND DISINFORMATION

W
E HAVE SHOWN THAT ALL OF THE CHARGES that the BDS movement levels against Israel are false. But how they advance those charges on the global media stage is just as important. The BDS movement is waging an ideological war, a war that is seeking to convince people around the world that Israel is a pariah among nations, deserving of economic and political isolation and—eventually—destruction.

Who are the people who buy into BDS rhetoric? First are those who are uninterested in the truth because they agree with the movement's ultimate goal. They agree, in other words, because their basic religious or political beliefs include the fervent desire to oppose, undermine, or destroy the Jewish state. Second are those who lack basic knowledge of the history and situation in the region, and who are influenced by politicians, entertainers, media, or friends with passionate anti-Israel views.

Meanwhile, there are people who are ideologically in tune with the BDS movement, but who still need to be convinced that isolating Israel is the best way to help Palestinians.

BDS campaigns seek to simultaneously whip up support of the first group, while persuading the others. The tactic they have embraced to accomplish this goal is called "disinformation." To understand the genesis of this method, it's essential to read Ion Pacepa's book *Disinformation*.[83] Pacepa was the head of Romania's spy agency, a top-ranking member of the KGB's inner circle, and responsible for, among other things, running disinformation operations. He is the most senior intelligence official ever to defect from the KGB's inner group and the only expert willing to divulge KGB protocols.

---

83 Supra, Pacepa and Rychlak

"Disinformation" is not "misinformation." Misinformation is the blunt instrument of propaganda: lies promulgated by a government—or nongovernmental organization—calculated to mislead people into false beliefs. For example, if the Iranian government published a report "proving" that its nuclear weapons program was peaceful, that would be misinformation. People interested in the truth, and with any knowledge of the Iranians' conduct since 1979, would reject that out of hand. Only people who had other religious or political reasons to accept the report would believe it.

But what if a dozen American newspapers decided to publish the report? Then it would become *disinformation,* because the falsehood would have been reported as truth.[84]

Every time the BDS movement's proponents accuse Israel of racism, apartheid, ethnic cleansing, war crimes, and genocide, they are trolling for people who might be convinced of the lies and who will repeat them to other audiences.

First in the propagation of the BDS movement's lies are the NGOs, many of which are Arab and Palestinian organizations, and those—like the many European organizations that fund the BDS movement (discussed below)—that have a pro-Palestinian and anti-Israel ideological bent. The second consists of other audiences susceptible to propaganda, including academia and the media. To reach them has been easy for the BDS movement.

Disinformation against Israel has roots predating the BDS movement. Long before the Durban NGO Forum, it was a weapon in ideological warfare. Indeed, since the Israeli military victory in 1967, the most productive atmosphere for disinformation campaigns attacking Israel has been the United Nations and its many platforms for activism.

In *Disinformation,* General Pacepa and coauthor Ronald Rychlak reveal that the Kremlin, at the direction of then–Soviet leader Yuri Andropov, used the United Nations to officially make anti-Semitism an international movement.[85] Supposedly the idea of the Arab bloc, the resolution was drafted in the Kremlin and supported by round-the-clock

---

[84] Id., p. 35
[85] Id., p. 276

disinformation operations. It was enthusiastically supported by Arafat, Fidel Castro, and most of the Soviet satellite nations in addition to the Arab nations.

Pacepa described how disinformation was an intelligence tool that the Soviets turned against Israel:

> Until 1972, the main task of the dezinformatsiya [disinformation] machinery was to change Europe's old hatred for the Nazis into a hatred for Zionist America, the new occupation power. In other words, to costume the Cold War in the robes of anti-Semitism in order to scare Europe and the rest of the world into believing that America wanted to transform it into a Zionist realm financed by Jewish money and run by a rapacious "Council of the Elders of Zion" (the Kremlin's epithet for the U.S. Congress). To get that image across, we were tasked to portray everyone and everything in America as being subordinated to Jewish interests: the leaders, the government, the political parties, the most prominent person-alities—and even American history.[86]

Pacepa cannot say that the BDS movement is connected to what is now Vladimir Putin's FSB, the successor to the KGB. But Pacepa said that there are similarities in what BDS is doing to a classical disinfor-mation campaign:

> In my view, the BDS tasks look like updated versions of the tasks the PLO had during the years I was still at the head of the dezinfor-matsiya machinery: to build anti-Semitism and anti-Americanism into an armed doctrine for the whole Palestinian world, as Mos-cow had built Marxism into an armed doctrine for the whole of Soviet bloc. At that time we branded Zionism as "a form of rac-ism and racial discrimination," and we equated it with Nazism. The tasks of today's BDS is to portray Israel as being an apartheid society as South Africa was before that system was swept away by Nelson Mandela (who was a member of the Communist Party).

---

86 Email interview with Pacepa, February 23, 2014

That there is no proof of a connection between the Russian FSB and the BDS movement is irrelevant. What is important is that the BDS movement has been closely patterned upon the model and strategy of prior disinformation campaigns. When we examine the facts, we see that the BDS movement satisfies the three criteria that define disinformation campaigns.

The first is that a disinformation campaign has to be based on lies. As we've demonstrated, the basis of BDS is false. The second is that the campaign must intend substantial harm to the target. Further, the harm is brought about indirectly; e.g., not by way of revolution, foreign military action, diplomacy, or other open means. That is BDS's methodology.

The third criterion is that a disinformation campaign has to be carried out intensively by a widespread network of people and organizations. Pacepa and Rychlak emphasize again and again how many people a disinformation campaign requires. During the Cold War, more people worked on disinformation campaigns than were in the Soviet army and the Soviet defense industry combined.[87] They were diplomats, government officials, intelligence agents, and all the allies that could be seduced to help.

The BDS movement easily satisfies that criterion as well. There isn't paperwork that shows that the BDS movement is a disinformation campaign carried on by old Soviet apparatchiks. But it is correct to say that those who lead the BDS movement have adopted the same tactics and strategy that were used by the Soviet intelligence community.

Rather than armies of pro-Soviet propagandists, the BDS campaign enlists the same huge network of NGOs that put on the NGO Forum at the Durban conference, along with the Palestinian activist organizations, many Arab nations, and their allies in Western nations. As we shall show below, it is Palestinian activist organizations and their allies who are operating the BDS movement's disinformation campaign.

---

[87] Supra, Pacepa and Rychlak, p. 38

CHAPTER 4

THE INTERNATIONAL
BDS MOVEMENT

BDS HAS FOUND A WELCOMING HOME in some European governments, in NGOs, and among a growing number of supporters around the world. That support needs to be understood in the context and terms of its supporters in the media.

The BDS movement appeals naturally to the majority of the global media, playing into the liberal sensibilities of most journalists. It is as *Washington Post* book editor Maria Arana said in 2005:

> The elephant in the newsroom is our narrowness. Too often, we wear liberalism on our sleeve and are intolerant of other lifestyles and opinions.... We're not very subtle about it at this paper: If you work here, you must be one of us. You must be liberal, progressive, a Democrat. I've been in communal gatherings in The Post, watching election returns, and have been flabbergasted to see my colleagues cheer unabashedly for the Democrats.[88]
>
> Media liberalism is accepted in the U.S. as the norm. It's neither a shock to those it affects, nor is it given much conscious thought. In a word, it's not a conspiracy: it's a culture.

That culture is found in most newsrooms throughout the Western world, deeply embedded in networks and newsrooms such as the BBC and the *New York Times*. It is the reason the media will report eagerly on the action of a Dutch pension manager to divest itself from Israeli banks but will leave almost completely unreported the fact that a wealthy

---

88 *Washington Post*, October 3, 2005

Chinese businessman would donate $130 million to create a partnership with an Israeli university.[89]

In parallel evolution, different species develop the same traits. Because it takes place in politics as well as in biology, the NGO community has developed the same sort of culture as the media. That culture dominates the NGO community for three important reasons.

First, the NGO community is composed primarily of groups that wish to take a supranational approach, claim to embrace altruistic principles, and thus generate a smoke screen behind which they can engage in political activism. (This distinguishes NGOs such as the International Committee of the Red Cross, which, although it sometimes falls into political activism, does not regularly engage in it.)

Thus, NGOs such as Amnesty International—which has a virulently anti-Israel track record stretching back to the 2001 Durban NGO Forum and before—states:

> Amnesty International is a global movement of more than 3 million supporters, members and activists in over 150 countries and territories who campaign to end grave abuses of human rights. Our vision is for every person to enjoy all the rights enshrined in the Universal Declaration of Human Rights and other international human rights standards.[90]

Second, what Amnesty International values above anything else is the "halo effect" that results from the supposed dedication to such lofty supranational missions and purposes. This halo surrounds its actions, regardless of their anti-Israeli bias and wrongheadedness, with an aura of beneficence as would befit the Little Sisters of the Poor. But like many similar NGOs, such as Human Rights Watch, the halo is misplaced. Too many groups like Amnesty and HRW take advantage of the halo to pursue an anti-Israel and pro-BDS agenda, and many European nations, as well as the European Union, generously fund them. As Professor Gerald Steinberg, president of NGO Monitor, has said, "Taxpayer money

---

89 http://www.jns.org/latest-articles/2013/10/6/bds-antidote-may-come-from-china#.U2VK2pvLwgQ

90 http://www.amnesty.org/en/who-we-are

is being channeled to organizations and activities that fuel the conflict, in violation of democratic principles. The EU can make a positive contribution to Israeli-Palestinian peace, but this requires a basic change in funding for radical NGOs."[91]

Third, the anti-Israel culture of the NGOs is contagious. Again, this is not a conspiracy, but it may have the same effect. NGOs, like other political entities, flock together like ducks on a pond. And when the common cause is Israel, the ducks find a lot of donors throwing them bread. In sum, the NGOs' culture is anti-Israeli because it is encouraged to be so by their donors, by many other members of the NGO community, and by the basic beliefs of their staffs.

The NGO-media analogy is precise. As L. Brent Bozell III, founder and president of the U.S. media watchdog Media Research Center, explained to us:

> The leftist bias in the U.S., indeed in the Western media, cannot be explained as the product of some nefarious conspiracy. It is a cultural hostility, an objection to American exceptionalism in all its forms and, by extension, to America's allies. Israel is not just America's steadfast neighbor in the Middle East, she is the epicenter of the Judeo-Christian tradition on which America was formed. Thus the hostility toward Israel, and the embrace of her enemies.

The same cultural bias is found in most of the NGO community. If you survey the NGOs, as NGO Monitor does regularly, you will find a commonality of anti-Israel and pro-BDS action and bias like that of Amnesty International that goes back at least as far as the 2001 Durban NGO Forum.[92] It's a shared culture that comforts its adherents in commonality. The Israelis surely know this, but they should recognize it and debate it publicly.

Aside from the NGOs, the anti-Israel culture is also en vogue among politicians in Europe and elsewhere, with a few notable exceptions like British Prime Minister David Cameron. In his first visit to Israel since

---

91 http://www.breitbart.com/Breitbart-London/2014/02/19/EU-Sponsoring-NGOs-Involved-in-anti-Israeli-Activities

92 http://www.ngo-monitor.org/index.php

becoming prime minister in March 2014, Cameron delivered a very tough speech to the Israeli parliament—the Knesset—in which he slammed BDS.

Cameron said, "Britain opposes boycotts, whether it's trade unions campaigning for the exclusion of Israelis or universities trying to stifle academic exchange." He said that delegitimizing Israel was "abhorrent" and promised that "together" Britain and Israel "would defeat it."[93] These remarks paint a sharp contrast between Cameron and Obama, and between Britain and most of Europe. (Though Cameron may not be aware of it, offices in his government, such as the British Department for Business Innovation and Skills, are contributing to BDS funding.[94])

In Europe, as we shall see, the BDS movement has had enormous success in securing funds directly and indirectly from governments and NGOs. In some places, even businesses have joined the BDS campaign. A particular case in point is the Netherlands. In January 2014, PGGM—a major Dutch fund manager—announced that it would divest from five Israeli banks because of their alleged involvement with the Israeli settlements in the West Bank. The investments (in the Bank Hapoalim, Bank Leumi, the First International Bank of Israel, Israel Discount Bank, and Mizrahi Tefahot Bank) were reportedly valued at tens of millions of euros.[95]

There is another aspect of the BDS movement's success in Europe. In June 2013, the European Commission issued guidelines that block EU grants, prizes, and funding for any Israeli entities in "occupied" Palestinian lands.[96] It is reasonable for the Israelis to fear that this action is a precursor to a broader EU boycott of Israeli businesses and institutions in compliance with the BDS movement's goals.

But BDS also has its detractors in Europe. In France, 12 pro-boycott activists were convicted of inciting racial hatred after they entered a

---

93 http://www.ft.com/intl/cms/s/0/901cdbbc-a9f9-11e3-adab-00144feab7de.html?siteedition=intl#axzz2vle87E9b

94 http://www.thecommentator.com/article/3544/revealed_british_government_funds_israel_boycott_activists

95 http://www.reuters.com/article/2014/01/08/netherlands-israel-divestment-idUSL6N0KI1N220140108

96 http://www.ft.com/intl/cms/s/0/96304cdc-ee01-11e2-816e-00144feabdc0.html#axzz30gX8AOB8

grocery store and applied yellow stickers with anti-Israel slogans to vegetables imported from Israel. France, which has a large and unassimilated Muslim population, has also banned a tour by an anti-Israel and anti-Semitic comedian, Dieudonne M'bala M'bala, who has frequently been convicted of belittling the Holocaust and contending that a Jewish mafia runs France.[97]

In Germany, the BDS movement hasn't had much effect. Although it has associated itself with various protests against Israel—advocating, for example, no further sale to Israel of German-made submarines—the protests haven't resulted in the action sought (or much else).[98]

In the Galician region of northwest Spain, five local trade unions voted to support the BDS movement.[99] That is not significant but, as we shall see, the Spanish government's financial support for BDS is.

In Australia, which apparently wants little to do with the entire array of Palestinian issues, the BDS movement seems to have been reduced to one blog that carries on about the political orientation of *The Australian* newspaper.[100]

China—which would not be expected to readily align itself with U.S. allies such as Israel—may have delivered the movement a crushing blow when one of its wealthiest businessmen gave an Israeli university a huge donation. Li Ka-Shing reportedly donated $130 million to Israel's Technion University. Li's gift was made "as part of a joint venture with Shantou University that will establish the Technion Guangdong Institute of Technology (TGIT)."[101]

The failure of the latest round of peace talks between Israelis and Palestinians will set off another large effort of the BDS movement. On April 3, 2014, speaking in Rabat, Secretary of State Kerry warned that he was about to reevaluate what was and wasn't possible in the

---

97 http://www.haaretz.com/jewish-world/1.574361

98 http://www.bdsmovement.net/2014/german-peace-groups-oppose-further-war-ships-to-israel-11592

99 http://www.theyeshivaworld.com/news/headlines-breaking-stories/154193/spanish-trade-unions-announce-support-for-anti-israel-bds-movement.html

100 http://australianbdscampaign.wordpress.com/

101 http://www.algemeiner.com/2013/10/08/solution-to-bds-movement-may-come-from-china/

negotiations and stated that the U.S. was unwilling to carry on negotiations indefinitely.[102]

The BDS movement will inevitably try to place blame for the talks' failure on Israel and use that failure to propel its disinformation campaign. The movement's supporters in the NGO community and within the Palestinian activist community will see their successes—in Spanish government support, in Dutch disinvestment of Israeli banks and more—and work persistently and energetically to capitalize on them.

It would be wrong to measure the threat of the BDS movement only in terms of its successes so far. Though they are considerable, the movement will continue as long as its funding lasts. As we shall see, that funding appears to be an increasing stream. As noted above, Israel's finance ministry has already declined to publish a report on the BDS movement's impact on the Israeli economy.[103] It would not have done so if the impact were trivial.

---

[102] http://www.globalsecurity.org/military/library/news/2014/04/mil-140404-vor03. htm?_m=3n%2e002a%2e1078%2egk0ao05n2l%2ezk4

[103] http://www.economist.com/news/middle-east-and-africa/21595948-israels-politicians-sound-rattled-campaign-isolate-their-country

CHAPTER 5

BDS IN AMERICA

THE BDS MOVEMENT HASN'T HAD MUCH LUCK in convincing Americans, at least outside of academia, to join in its boycott of Israel. It is difficult to see why they have been relatively successful even among the colleges and universities.

The simple fact is that while the BDS movement claims that its boycott would extend academic freedom, in fact it would do the opposite. In his book, Barghouti castigates the American Association of University Professors (AAUP), which declined to follow the example of the British Association of University Teachers in boycotting some or all Israeli schools.

Barghouti argues: "By positioning its particular notion of academic freedom as being of 'paramount importance,' the AAUP effectively, if not intentionally, sharply limits the moral obligations of scholars in responding to situations of oppression."[104] What this means is that academic freedom does not include freedom of thought and scholarship—and should be limited to studies consistent with the ideology of the BDS movement.

Contrast that with what AAUP said:

Since its founding in 1915, the AAUP has been committed to preserving and advancing the free exchange of ideas among academics irrespective of governmental policies and however unpalatable those policies may be viewed. We reject proposals that curtail the freedom of teachers and researchers to engage in work with academic colleagues, and we reaffirm the paramount importance of the freest possible international movement of scholars and ideas.[105]

---

104 Supra, Barghouti, p. 87
105 http://www.aaup.org/report/academic-boycotts

The AAUP's stand is simple and correct: Barghouti and the BDS movement are trying to impose their own limitations on academic freedom and thereby destroy it.

In December 2013, the American Studies Association voted to support the BDS academic boycott. Its resolution for the boycott said, in part:

> Whereas the American Studies Association is committed to the pursuit of social justice, to the struggle against all forms of racism, including anti-Semitism, discrimination, and xenophobia, and to solidarity with aggrieved peoples in the United States and in the world...
>
> It is resolved that the American Studies Association (ASA) endorses and will honor the call of Palestinian civil society for a boycott of Israeli academic institutions. It is also resolved that the ASA supports the protected rights of students and scholars everywhere to engage in research and public speaking about Israel-Palestine and in support of the boycott, divestment, and sanctions (BDS) movement.[106]

The reaction to the ASA's resolution was quick and severe. Eighty U.S. college presidents—including presidents of many of the best U.S. universities and colleges—condemned the ASA's action as contrary to academic freedom. According to a *New York Times* report, at least five universities quit the ASA over it: Bard College, Brandeis University, Indiana University, Kenyon College, and the Pennsylvania State University at Harrisburg. That report quotes Carolyn Martin, president of Amherst College, as saying, "Such boycotts threaten academic speech and exchange, which it is our solemn duty as academic institutions to protect."[107]

Part of the reason that the ASA's action hasn't been significant is the organization's size. The ASA has approximately 5,000 members, of whom only about 1,200 voted for the resolution.[108] In contrast, the American

---

[106] http://www.theasa.net/american_studies_association_resolution_on_academic_boycott_of_israel

[107] http://www.nytimes.com/2014/01/06/us/backlash-against-israel-boycott-throws-academic-association-on-defensive.html

[108] http://www.maannews.net/eng/ViewDetails.aspx?ID=657570

Association of University Professors—which has rejected the academic boycott—has about 47,000 members.

Aside from the ASA's action, and some student demonstrations in favor of a boycott, the BDS movement hasn't had much success in gaining American sympathy, at least outside the White House. Coca Cola has indirectly supported BDS by donating more than $2.5 million to Oxfam International, which has demonstrated itself to be an anti-Israeli NGO.[109]

Part of the difficulty BDS is having in gaining American adherents stems from the character of their advocates here. Barghouti—the holder of a master's degree from Tel Aviv University—is hardly a credible source for the accusation that Israel is an "apartheid" state. Worse still is the Council on American-Islamic Relations (CAIR), which tries to pass itself off as a civil rights organization.

You might expect that any organization that wants to qualify itself as a civil rights defender would support women and condemn the crimes of "honor killings" and genital mutilation that they suffer in much of the Islamic world. Not CAIR.

In April, CAIR managed to shut down the showing of *Honor Diaries*, a movie that profiles nine women and their experiences with "honor killings," "honor violence," genital mutilation, and forced marriage. They did so on the grounds that it constituted "Islamophobia."[110] To CAIR, it's "Islamophobic" to condemn crimes against women in Islamic nations.

CAIR is an organization firmly in the fold of the Muslim Brotherhood and whose agenda is coordinated with several other such organizations.[111] The Muslim Brotherhood was designated a terrorist organization by the Saudi Arabian government in March 2014.[112]

CAIR, along with the National Lawyers Guild (NLG) and the Center for Constitutional Rights (CCR), came out with a letter opposing the anti-BDS Lipinski-Roskam (HR-4009) bill as soon as it was

---

109 http://freebeacon.com/coke-backs-bds-group-trying-to-cripple-israeli-soda-competitor/

110 http://www.foxnews.com/opinion/2014/03/31/islamophobia-in-action-honor-diaries-screening-shut-down-by-cair/

111 Andrew McCarthy, "The Grand Jihad," pp. 150–155

112 http://www.defensenews.com/article/20140224/DEFREG04/302240014/Palestinian-BDS-Threat-Hangs-Above-Negotiations

introduced in Congress.[113] The NLG and the CCR are hard-left radical groups. CAIR's sorry history includes the fact that several of its key members have been convicted of federal felonies, including terrorism offenses.[114]

At this juncture, it appears that the BDS movement in America is growing slowly and with increasing effect in the colleges and universities, just as the antiwar movement did in the 1960s and 1970s. It has the potential to become very large, for many of the same reasons the antiwar movement did.

Men and women of college age are often more passionate about politics and more open to new trends of thought than older people. Idealism is one of their greatest virtues. Given the fact that most faculties are overwhelmingly liberal, the faculties' attitudes and peer groups can—as they did in the antiwar movement—ignite protests and even propel them to national attention. When you add to that faculty members who are pro-BDS activists, the result is inevitable.

Corey Robin is one such teacher. He's a political science professor at Brooklyn College and the City University of New York Graduate Center.[115] His writing is tedious and long-winded, and his support for the BDS movement is strong. Here is Robin writing about a criticism of BDS in *The New Republic:*

> But it's Kazin's final point about the "flashy" politics of the BDS movement as against the connected criticism of economic justice movements that I find hardest to understand. For starters, most of the activists around BDS that I know are also involved in economic justice campaigns. Take the activist I know best: me. I first got involved in the left through my work with a TA union in the 1990s, and I've continued to be involved in various campus labor activities since then. I also support BDS. And I know lots of people like me....

---

[113] https://ccrjustice.org/newsroom/press-releases/ccr,-nlg-and-cair-usa-ask-house-education-committee-oppose-anti-boycott-bill

[114] Supra, McCarthy, pp. 152-153

[115] http://coreyrobin.com/about/

When Kazin describes connected criticism by citing Walzer—challenging "the leaders, the conventions, the ritual practices of a particular society ... in the name of values recognized and shared in the same society"—I think he's actually describing the BDS movement quite well. Most BDS activists I know speak on behalf of the most minimal norms of a liberal democracy, which are widely shared in the U.S.: namely, that Israel should be the state of its citizens (and not some far-flung community of an ancient diaspora), and that it should govern itself according to the norms of one person/one vote, as opposed to the hard facts of ethnic privilege and military occupation.[116]

Teachers like Robin produce students like Robin. And around the nation, students like Robin are demonstrating support for BDS.

The organization Students for Justice in Palestine (SJP) is one of several propelling these actions. Their website brags of divestment resolutions passed by students at the University of California–Irvine, UC Berkeley, UC San Diego, Oberlin College, and Arizona State University. Praising a resolution passed by students at Loyola University in Chicago, the SJP wrote,

There would be no Loyola Chicago today without the birth of a first-century Palestinian from Bethlehem named Jesus. If Jesus were to attempt to minister between Bethlehem and Jerusalem in the modern-day Holy Land, he would be confronted with multiple illegal Israeli military checkpoints and a 30 ft. high concrete barrier.[117]

They seem to have flunked the classes in history and religion in which they should have learned that Jesus was a Jew.

Another pro-BDS student group is Students Allied for Freedom and Equality (SAFE). In December 2013, SAFE delivered mock eviction notices to students at the University of Michigan at Ann Arbor purportedly from the university's housing authority, threatening demolition of the students' premises. The notices were followed by a *Michigan Daily*

---

116 http://coreyrobin.com/2013/12/13/a-response-to-michael-kazin-on-bds-and-campus-activism/

117 http://sjpnational.org/

Viewpoint article telling students that the eviction notices were political satire and asking them to join the BDS movement.[118]

In March 2014, when the university's student senate was going to vote on a divestment resolution, pro-BDS activists shouted death threats at one student. As the *Washington Free Beacon* reported:

> The pro-Israel student received death threats and ... others have allegedly been called "kikes" and "dirty Jews" by backers of the virulently anti-Israel Boycott, Divestment, and Sanctions (BDS) movement, which aims to delegitimize the Jewish state through economic means.[119]

The BDS movement is using social media—Twitter, Facebook, Tumblr, and the like—to gain traction on more campuses. The BDS Support Network Facebook page says its object is to assist activists worldwide in setting up campaigns.[120] That Facebook page has over 20,000 "likes" worldwide. Similar is the BDS movement's Twitter feed, which has about 17,500 followers. The End the Occupation website features a map of the national BDS campaigns, of which there are many.[121] These social media vehicles are providing powerful organizational tools for the BDS movement in America, enabling coordination of protest demonstrations, petition drives, and much more.

Whether the BDS movement will have success outside of academia is impossible to say. But given its abilities to gain publicity, it cannot be discounted as a force in American politics.

---

118 http://www.algemeiner.com/2013/12/17/anti-israel-hate-speech-and-slander-at-the-university-of-michigan-%E2%80%8E%E2%80%8E%E2%80%8E/

119 http://freebeacon.com/issues/pro-israel-students-called-kike-dirty-jew-at-university-of-michigan/

120 https://www.facebook.com/BDSSupportNetwork/info

121 http://www.endtheoccupation.org/article.php?id=3383

CHAPTER 6

WHO FUNDS
THE BDS MOVEMENT?

O N OCTOBER 8, 1997, THE U.S. STATE DEPARTMENT designated several Palestinian groups as foreign terrorist organizations.
Among those groups are Hamas, The Popular Front for the Liberation
of Palestine (PFLP), Palestinian Islamic Jihad, the Palestine Liberation
Front, and the PFLP General Command.[122] Those designations remain
in place today.

Among the NGOs most actively supporting the BDS movement is
the Coalition of Women for Peace (CWP), whose website describes it
as "a feminist organization against the occupation of Palestine and for
a just peace."[123] Members of CWP have participated in events in which
they carried the flag of the PFLP terrorist group.[124]

One of the main sources of funding for CWP, if not the single greatest source, is the European Union. Through the European Instrument
for Human Rights and Democracy (EIHRD), the EU donated more
money—about €11 million from 2007 to 2010 alone—to support the Palestinians' political agenda than to groups in any other part of the world.[125]

EIHRD is one of the most anti-Israel sources of NGO funding. It
ignores other regions and issues with legitimate human rights problems
and instead gives most of its money to groups supporting BDS. According to Professor Gerald Steinberg, president of NGO Monitor, EIHRD
has "allocated over 11 million euros to NGOs in Israel and the Palestinian Authority, which represents 57% of EIHRD funding directed at the

122   http://www.state.gov/j/ct/rls/other/des/123085.htm

123   http://www.coalitionofwomen.org/?page_id=340&lang=en

124   http://www.jpost.com/Opinion/Op-Ed-Contributors/Why-does-the-EU-continue-
to-fund-anti-peace-NGOs-341129

125   Id.

Middle East, while projects in Syria, Iraq, Iran, Oman, Saudi Arabia, and the UAE are largely ignored by such EU frameworks."[126]

The most telling comment about EIHRD's deep involvement in funding pro-BDS groups comes from the EU itself. Leonello Gabrici, who is a senior EU official of the European Union External Action Service, said, "We are not working on boycotting Israel but rather on preparing an unprecedented package of EU-added value for peace."[127]

Gabrici speaks from inside the anti-Israel cultural bubble. To him, the only "EU-added value" that could promote peace is investment in pro-Palestinian groups. Like many others who inhabit the NGO cultural bubble, he is willing to ignore the very worst human rights violations in countries such as Iran, Iraq, Saudi Arabia, North Korea, and the like in order to feed the anti-Israel movement. .

The EU is not alone. Many European nations fund the BDS movement generously. The Spanish government, for example, has donated millions of euros to anti-Israel NGOs. From 2009 to 2011 it donated about €1.12 million to the Applied Research Institute for Jerusalem, about €380,000 to Breaking the Silence, and about €107,000 to the Popular Struggle Coordination Committee.[128] Meanwhile, the Swedish government contributes directly to radical Palestinian organizations in Sweden through its Swedish International Development Cooperation Agency (SIDA).[129]

The Swedish NGO Diakonia is of particular interest. In 2008, Diakonia had a budget of about $47.2 million, 90 percent of which was provided by the Swedish government.[130] According to NGO Monitor, Diakonia has adopted both the Palestinians' positions and their tactics, including its use of "lawfare."[131]

Lawfare is a tactic that uses a nation's legal system to achieve political or even military ends contrary to the nation's interests and frequently by

---

[126] http://www.breitbart.com/Breitbart-London/2014/02/19/EU-Sponsoring-NGOs-Involved-in-anti-Israeli-Activities

[127] Id.

[128] http://unitedwithisrael.org/spanish-government-funds-anti-israel-ngos/

[129] http://www.israelnationalnews.com/Articles/Article.aspx/14350#.UyR2oJvLwgR

[130] http://www.ngo-monitor.org/article/diakonia

[131] Id.

litigation. According to The Lawfare Project, the goals of lawfare include preventing the application of human rights laws where they are needed most, confusing the laws of war with human rights law, and to silence and punish free speech about national security issues.[132]

In some infamous examples, lawfare is often used to suppress legitimate debate, even to suppress the publication of books that expose the terrorism-related motivations of the subjects. In one case, the 2006 book *Alms for Jihad,* by J. Millard Burr and Robert Collins, was published by Cambridge University Press. The book analyzes, in great detail, the funding of terrorism through Islamic charities. The book prominently mentions Sheikh Khalid bin Mahfouz, a Saudi businessman who was also a banker to the Saudi royal family. When Mahfouz sued for libel in a British court, the authors and the publisher were faced with the backward principles of British libel law. Instead of the plaintiffs having to prove the falsity of the allegations in the book, as they would in American courts, the defendants were required to prove their truth, which is the opposite of the burden of proof in American libel cases.

Facing condemnation from many members of the Muslim community in Britain and a hugely expensive legal battle, the publisher settled the case by withdrawing the work and destroying all the unsold copies as well as paying Mahfouz an undisclosed amount.[133] There have been several other cases of "libel tourism" like the Mahfouz case, in which libel plaintiffs can forum shop to enter British courts.

In 2009, Diakonia notoriously submitted a report to Goldstone's U.N. investigation of the Gaza incursion that vilified Israel and tried to delegitimize its ability to defend itself from rocket attacks.[134]

Spain and Sweden aren't the only governments that fund the jungle of NGOs that, in turn, fund the BDS movement and engage in political activism on its behalf. Among those supporting the cause directly or indirectly are the Netherlands, Germany, Canada, and Ireland.[135]

---

132 http://www.thelawfareproject.org/what-is-lawfare.html

133 http://www.nytimes.com/2007/10/07/books/review/Donadio-t.html?pagewanted=all&_r=0

134 Id.

135 http://www.ngo-monitor.org/article/the_boycott_industry_background_information_and_analysis_on_bds_campaigns

To discover the governments and NGOs that fund the BDS movement, you have to dig deeply, because it has become an elaborate network akin to a money-laundering scheme. This represents a deliberate effort to provide donors a level of plausible deniability while still enabling donors to support the goals and ideology of the BDS movement. That money laundering enables donors to avoid being identified with the calumnies the BDS movement regularly launches against Israel.

Consider Oxfam, an international organization whose stated mission is to work with partner organizations and alongside vulnerable women to end the causes of poverty.[136] But Oxfam's actual role has, like that of many "halo NGOs," devolved into political activism. Thus, for example, Oxfam recently demanded that actress Scarlett Johansson—an "Oxfam ambassador"—withdraw from participation in an advertising campaign for SodaStream, an Israeli company that has a facility in the West Bank.[137]

Oxfam claims it doesn't fund the BDS movement's activities. But it does fund the CWP organization, which takes a very active role in BDS, to the point of carrying the flag of a terrorist organization in a demonstration. [138]

This is how the NGOs keep their halos. Money is fungible: one donation cannot be traced to any specific organization's being funded and especially not to a specific activity of that organization. So Oxfam can support the BDS movement's goals, initiatives, and ideology without leaving its fingerprints on organizations like CWP. A few examples will illustrate how the money laundering works, and how it allows the governments and NGOs involved to pretend they aren't actively involved in the campaign to delegitimize Israel. In Appendix A, we've set forth an NGO Monitor chart that shows much of the European funding for the BDS campaign passes through NGOs that are actively working to support it. Some governments, like the Netherlands, are apparently proud

---

[136] http://www.oxfam.org/en/about

[137] http://www.nydailynews.com/entertainment/scarlett-johansson-stepping-oxfam-ambassador-article-1.1596338

[138] http://www.ngo-monitor.org/article/the_boycott_industry_background_information_and_analysis_on_bds_campaigns

of the support they give the BDS movement. Others, such as Norway, work hard to hide it.

The Al Mezan Center for Human Rights, located in the Gaza Strip, has endorsed the BDS movement's 2005 "call to action" against Israel.[139] It receives funding from the Palestinian NGO Development Center ($425,000 in 2010–2012); Sweden (€105,000 in 2007–2009); Trocaire, an Irish charity, in an unknown amount; and both Norway and the EU, both in undisclosed amounts. Al Mezan issues reports on Israel's "siege" of the Gaza Strip and holds "educational" sessions on such topics.[140] It is, as may be seen from its press releases, generating publicity useful only to the BDS movement and the terrorist organization Hamas.[141]

The Applied Research Institute in Jerusalem (ARIJ) is another NGO that endorses the BDS movement and all its baggage.[142] In 2011, it received $645,000 from Spain, $75,200 from the United Kingdom, $534,745 from the EU, $1,389,503 from Sweden, and $44,795 from DanChurchAid in Denmark, for a total of $2,689,243.

According to its 2011 annual report:

> In the geopolitical arena, ARIJ continued monitoring Israeli activities and documenting Israeli violations in the Occupied Palestinian Territories, in addition to raising awareness through the use of all kinds of publications, audio and visual dialogue interviews; one important aspect is the production of short videos on ARIJ YouTube account and daily report.[143]
>
> In short, some large portion of ARIJ's programming is intended to produce information that will be useful to the BDS movement.

Even the most radical, such as the Coalition of Women for Peace, has a steady stream of generous funding (see Appendix A). Included

---

139 Supra, Barghouti, p. 244

140 See, e.g., http://www.mezan.org/en/details.php?id=18411&ddname=report&id_dept=14&id2=9&p=center

141 http://www.mezan.org/en/center.php?id_dept=9

142 Supra, Barghouti, p. 244

143 http://www.arij.org/files/ARIJ_Annual_Report_2011-small1.pdf

in its funding in 2013 were donations from: Oxfam Novib (Netherlands) ($117,421), ICCO (Netherlands) ($110,513), NOVACT (Spain, UNDP) ($69,002), EED (Germany) ($34,644), Medico International (Germany) ($13,814), Kvinna Till Kvinna (Sweden) ($13,676), The United Church of Canada ($9,946), and Trocaire (Ireland) ($6,891), for a total of $375, 907.

MIFTAH is the creation of Hanan Ashrawi, a member of the Palestine Liberation Organization executive committee.[144] (The PLO Popular Committees in the West Bank and Gaza have endorsed the BDS movement's 2005 "call," as has MIFTAH.[145]) Ashrawi is a vocal supporter of the BDS movement. Her pro-BDS op-eds appear in Israeli newspapers.[146] Among its contributors in 2012 were the International Republican Institute in the U.S. ($154,457), Norway ($130,000), the Palestinian NGO Development Center ($130,000), the United Nations Development Program ($70,477), Ireland ($66,680), the Konrad Adenauer Stiftung ($44,702), and Oxfam Novib (Netherlands, $5,272).

Organizations such as Al Mezan, ARIJ, MIFTAH, CWP, and the rest are dedicated entirely to feeding the BDS disinformation machine. But what part of the funds donated to them by European governments, NGOs, and hidden donors goes directly to fund the BDS movement itself?

The funding cannot all come from the European NGOs and governments. Judging by the other manipulative strategies the Arab nations and others invest in heavily, it's practically a certainty that the governments of Saudi Arabia, Qatar (whose government runs the al-Jazeera international television network), and others are funding BDS. The Turks' loud support for the Palestinians—and the deaths of Turkish activists in the Mavi Marmara incident—make it reasonably certain that the Ergodan government is also helping fund BDS. And it would be a shock to find that the Iranians are not participating. At this point, there is no smoking gun tracing funds from Arab governments, Turkey, or Iran to BDS groups.[147] Their support for the

---

[144] http://www.haaretz.com/misc/writers/hanan-ashrawi-1.423863

[145] Supra, Barghouti, pp. 243, 245

[146] http://www.haaretz.com/opinion/.premium-1.573315

[147] The Im Tirtzu has a 2010 report on the subject that may be well-sourced, but the report itself includes a strong disclaimer of its accuracy (http://www.imti.org.il/Reports/WFTD_English_Report.pdf).

BDS movement, if any, remains the secret of the governments and the recipients. But given their hostility to Israel as expressed in the U.N. and elsewhere, it's only logical to assume that the funding exists, and that it is significant.

CHAPTER 7

IMPLICATIONS FOR UNITED STATES AND ISRAELI POLICY

THE BDS MOVEMENT'S EFFECTS on United States foreign and domestic policy can be divided into three periods: Bush's presidency, Obama's presidency, and post-Obama.

During the George W. Bush administration, from 2001 to 2009, BDS had no discernable effect on U.S. policy.

During the Obama administration, BDS has gained at least rhetorical traction, likely resulting from the president's apparent disdain for Israel and his personal animosity toward Israeli Prime Minister Netanyahu. In his 2009 Cairo speech, Obama spoke of Israel as America's ally. But he also said,

On the other hand, it is also undeniable that the Palestinian people—Muslims and Christians—have suffered in pursuit of a homeland. For more than 60 years they've endured the pain of dislocation. Many wait in refugee camps in the West Bank, Gaza, and neighboring lands for a life of peace and security that they have never been able to lead. They endure the daily humiliations—large and small—that come with occupation. So let there be no doubt: The situation for the Palestinian people is intolerable.[148]

As Obama's presidency unfolded, the approach of American policy toward Israel has evolved, demonstrating more rhetorical sympathy with BDS. Despite this, Obama hasn't and certainly won't adopt the BDS movement's goals as his own.

What Obama has done, and may well continue to do, is to shift American policy from strong support of Israel to diffidence and then to

---

148 http://www.whitehouse.gov/the_press_office/Remarks-by-the-President-at-Cairo-University-6-04-09

opposition. His initial stance, that of a supposedly impartial arbiter of the Israeli-Palestinian dispute, gradually tilted the negotiation table in the Palestinians' favor. Throughout his public career, Obama has demonstrated sympathy with the Palestinian cause, a position that is traceable to the influence of the late Edward Said.

Said was a Palestinian activist who became an American academic. His was a radical anticolonialist ideology that infused his writing, public utterances, and certainly his classroom. His book *Orientalism* is full of ideas such as this:

> The impact of colonialism, of worldly circumstances, of historical development: all these were to Orientalists as flies to wanton boys, killed—or disregarded—for their sport, never taken seriously enough to complicate the essential Islam.[149]

Said was a leading anticolonialist thinker in his time. Obama was a student of Said's at Columbia and maintained a relationship with him for two decades.[150]

In March 2010, angry about new Israeli settlements in the West Bank, Obama met with Netanyahu in the White House and presented him with a list of 13 demands, the key to which was the end of new settlements. Upon leaving the room, Obama reportedly admonished Netanyahu to consider the error of his ways, and told him he would "be around" if he wanted to call.[151] The two met later again that evening but did not heal their disagreement.

In May 2011, Obama outlined his plan for Israeli peace with the Palestinians. It was nothing new, requiring Israel to return to the pre-1967 war borders—which he knows Israel believes to be indefensible—with "land swaps" to accommodate specific settlements. He also warned that the Jewish state cannot permanently occupy Palestinian lands and said that the Palestinians deserve a sovereign and contiguous state of their

---

[149] Edward Said, "Orientalism," Vintage Books (1979), p. 106

[150] http://www.theblaze.com/contributions/edward-said-obamas-founding-father/

[151] http://www.telegraph.co.uk/news/worldnews/barackobama/7521220/Obama-snubbed-Netanyahu-for-dinner-with-Michelle-and-the-girls-Israelis-claim.html

own.[152] A "contiguous" Palestinian state could not be created without joining the Gaza Strip and the West Bank, cutting Israel in half.

In June 2013, Secretary of State Kerry told the AJC Global Forum, "Well, the difference is that what happens in the coming days will actually dictate what happens in the coming decades. We're running out of time. We're running out of possibilities. And let's be clear: If we do not succeed now—and I know I'm raising those stakes—but if we do not succeed now, we may not get another chance."[153]

Kerry's attitude, pushing hard for the plan Obama outlined in 2011, put enormous pressure on Israel to come to terms with the Palestinians even though the Palestinians' position was the same as it was in 2011, when Mahmoud Abbas said, "I've said it before and I'll say it again. I will never recognize the Jewishness of the state, or a 'Jewish state.'"[154]

This brought about an unprecedented scolding of Kerry in January 2014 by Israeli Defense Minister Moshe Yaalon, who called Kerry's approach to the peace talks "messianic," declared that Kerry's peace plan wasn't worth the paper it was printed on, and opined that Kerry should take a Nobel Prize and go home.[155] At that point, the Obama-Kerry rhetoric shifted dramatically toward the Palestinian position, almost echoing BDS.

In February 2014, during a Munich meeting with his Iranian counterpart, Mohammed Zarif, Secretary of State Kerry seemed to call for the United States to align itself with BDS. It was also the time in which new European Union regulations were enacted, further restricting trade with Israel. Kerry said, "The risks are very high for Israel. People are talking about boycott. That will intensify in the case of failure. Do [the Israelis] want a failure that then begs whatever may come in the form of a response from disappointed Palestinians and the Arab community?"[156]

---

152 http://www.telegraph.co.uk/news/worldnews/barackobama/8525214/Barack-Obama-Israel-must-recognise-1967-borders.html

153 http://www.ajc.org/site/apps/nlnet/content2.aspx?c=7oJILSPwFfJSG&b=8712787 &ct=13168621

154 Supra, note 108

155 http://www.timesofisrael.com/defense-minister-reportedly-trashes-kerry-peace-talks/

156 http://www.telegraph.co.uk/news/worldnews/middleeast/israel/10613055/John-Kerry-labelled-anti-Semite-for-warning-of-possible-boycott-of-Israel.html

With that remark, Kerry came very close to joining the U.S. with those who advocate the boycott of Israel. His choice of venue for these remarks—a meeting with representatives of the nation that has vowed repeatedly to wipe Israel off the map—makes their impact that much worse.

In a March 2014 interview, President Obama went further, almost adopting some of the BDS movement's rhetoric: "There comes a point where you can't manage this anymore, and then you start having to make very difficult choices. Do you resign yourself to what amounts to a permanent occupation of the West Bank? Is that the character of Israel as a state for a long period of time? Do you perpetuate, over the course of a decade or two decades, more and more restrictive policies in terms of Palestinian movement? Do you place restrictions on Arab-Israelis in ways that run counter to Israel's traditions?"[157]

In that atmosphere, Obama's venture in the peace process failed.

The Peace Process

April 29 came and went, and no one was better or worse for its passing. Except, perhaps, President Obama who had set it as an artificial deadline for outlining a final agreement in the peace negotiations between Israel and the Palestinians.

The failure of Obama's effort was just another nonachievement to be added to his record as a statesman. Among Obama's nonachievements are the agreement by which Syria was to give up its chemical weapons (which it hasn't), the first stage of his nuclear agreement with Iran (which has only served to enable Iran to buy enough time to protect its regime and the means of delivering nuclear weapons before actually building a functioning warhead), and Russian President Putin's takeover of the Crimean Peninsula. (All of that came after the strategic arms limitation agreement with Putin, in which Obama agreed to reduce America's nuclear arsenal but also made what the Russians contend is a concession that had never been made before: that American missile defenses would count as offensive weapons.)

---

[157] http://www.bloombergview.com/articles/2014-03-02/obama-to-israel-time-is-running-out

Diplomacy, like politics, is an art that requires compromise. But the areas in which compromise can be reached are limited by what the parties believe are their vital interests. A nation such as Israel or a group such as the Palestinians can be induced by economic or military force to compromise a vital interest, but not otherwise. Nor are deadlines for compromise set by officious intermeddlers: real deadlines are set by facts on the ground as the parties to the dispute see them.

In this round of the peace process, Obama's deadline had to fail because neither party was required by the facts on the ground to concede any of what it believed to be its vital interests.

It is apparent that Secretary of State Kerry—with the president's approval—wants to blame Israel for the peace talks' failure. In a closed-door meeting of the Trilateral Commission on April 24, with the failure of the talks at hand, Kerry said that unless Israel agreed with the Palestinians soon to a two-state solution, it risked becoming an apartheid state.[158]

President Obama may still want to push the Israelis into more concessions, though he is unlikely to succeed. Obama's reputation as a statesman has been badly damaged by the failures catalogued above. For that reason alone, he may want to resurrect that reputation by pushing the Israelis even harder.

If Obama wants to try again, he may make another plan that will give the appearance of making end runs around the primary issues of the pre-1967 borders—to which the Israelis refuse to return, saying they are indefensible—and the so-called "right of return," which the Palestinians insist upon as a way to ensure that Israel's democracy can be destroyed.

That, too, is highly unlikely to happen, because the sudden announcement of a Fatah-Hamas reconciliation on April 23 will make it impossible for any agreement between Israel and the Palestinians. Though presidential adviser Philip Gordon reportedly told Jewish leaders that the announced reconciliation "wasn't necessarily a bad thing" and could strengthen Mahmoud Abbas's hand,[159] that is fundamentally wrong. Israel cannot negotiate with a government half of which is dedicated to Israel's destruction.

---

158 http://www.thedailybeast.com/articles/2014/04/27/exclusive-kerry-warns-israel-could-become-an-apartheid-state.html

159 http://www.haaretz.com/news/diplomacy-defense/.premium-1.587869

We know, from Barghouti's statement in a February 2010 interview that even if the Israelis pulled out of the West Bank entirely, the BDS movement would continue its attempted boycott because, in his view, Palestinians are still "oppressed" by the denial of their purported "right of return." [160] We also know, from Barghouti's book, that the BDS movement believes there cannot be coexistence with Israel:

'Talking' to Israelis, as in the flourishing 'peace' industry's dialogue groups, not only has been misleading and terribly harmful to the struggle for a just peace, giving the false impression that coexistence can be achieved despite Zionist oppression, but has also failed to bring about any positive shift in Israeli public opinion toward supporting justice as a condition for peace. [161]

In subsequent months, Obama will either throw his hands up and—like Kerry—blame Israel for the failure of the latest "peace plan" or decide to intervene personally and host meetings in hope of forcing a settlement. The former is most likely, because to intervene to that extent would attach some responsibility to Obama for the inevitable failure of the negotiations.

One can't overlook the impact of other Obama policies that have a negative effect on Israel. Obama's interim deal with Iran, which purports to prevent the development of Iranian nuclear weapons, essentially blocks any Israeli attack on Iran's nuclear weapons facilities. Israeli Prime Minister Netanyahu has, in two addresses to the U.N. General Assembly, given warning of the imminent danger of the Iranian nuclear program.

In Netanyahu's 2012 speech, he warned that Iran was within six or eight months of enriching enough uranium to build a nuclear weapon. He urged the U.N. to believe that time was running out and that the Iranians would soon pass the point at which a military strike would be able to deprive them of the ability to produce a nuclear weapon. That was September 2012. [162]

---

[160] https://www.youtube.com/watch?v=qOBg2t6vscc

[161] Supra, Barghouti, p. 147

[162] http://www.algemeiner.com/2012/09/27/full-transcript-prime-minister-netanyahu-speech-to-united-nations-general-assembly-2012-video/

In the 2011–2013 time frame, Israel repeatedly sought to buy large, deep-penetrating bunker buster bombs from the United States. Its requests were denied.[163]

In November 2013, Obama's deal with Iran was announced. The interim deal will last for six months, after which it can be extended. While it lasts, Israel's hands are tied. It cannot attack Iran, interfering in Obama's "peace process." Iran's intent to build nuclear weapons has been demonstrated for many years in its testing of nuclear triggers, its uranium enrichment, its acquisition of "heavy water," and more.[164] Obama's deal with Iran banks on the trustworthiness of the Iran kakistocracy. It's a bad bet for America, and a worse bet for Israel.

What America's post-Obama policy will be depends, obviously, on who is elected to succeed him. The only certainty is that if America's 45th president is Hillary Clinton, she will follow the path toward isolating and boycotting Israel that Obama has followed. In 1999, while First Lady, Clinton visited Yasser Arafat's wife, Suha, and in a joint appearance stood there while Mrs. Arafat accused the Israelis of using poison gas to attack Palestinians.[165] (Mrs. Clinton kissed Mrs. Arafat before that remark was made.)

Clinton's sympathies apparently continue to be with the Palestinians. In 2012, for example, she told a forum on U.S.-Israeli relations:

> So, look, I'm not making excuses for the missed opportunities of the Israelis, or the lack of generosity, the lack of empathy that I think goes hand-in-hand with the suspicion. So, yes, there is more that the Israelis need to do to really demonstrate that they do understand the pain of an oppressed people in their minds, and they want to figure out, within the bounds of security and a Jewish democratic state, what can be accomplished.[166]

---

163 http://www.worldtribune.com/2013/05/07/obama-three-times-denied-israels-request-for-mop-bunker-busters/

164 See, e.g., http://www.foxnews.com/story/2009/12/14/secret-document-exposes-iran-nuclear-trigger/ and http://www.jpost.com/Iranian-Threat/News/Report-Iran-Arak-facility-to-have-nuclear-weapons-grade-plutonium-by-next-summer-322093

165 http://www.nydailynews.com/archives/news/damage-control-hil-incident-arafat-wife-touches-furor-article-1.844809

166 http://www.breitbart.com/Big-Peace/2012/12/01/Hillary-rips-Israel

Who will be elected president in November 2016 is not something we can yet forecast. But if it is Hillary Clinton, what Obama began she will continue.

American policy should be something very different and so should Israel's.

The Future of U.S. Policy

In the post-Obama era, America must again make clear to the world—by actions, not just words—that Israel is its most valued ally in the Middle East. We need to cancel the nuclear deal with Iran and reimpose economic sanctions whether the rest of the world joins us or not. The remaining nations of the West will respond positively to American leadership.

America should sell to Israel whatever arms would enable it to destroy Iran's nuclear weapons facilities if such an attack is even possible by the time Obama leaves office. It may not be. If it is not, we will have to face the fact that there will be no peaceful way to prevent Iran from obtaining nuclear arms, and act accordingly.

Last, and not least, the next American president should condemn the BDS movement for what it says, and for its goals of delegitimizing and destroying Israel. There should be no doubt left—especially among the Palestinians—that their disinformation campaign has failed.

One way this should be done is for Congress to enact a bill like the 1976–1977 antiboycott legislation that defeated the Arab embargo. The 1976 Ribicoff amendment to the Tax Reform Act and the 1977 amendments to the Export Administration Act preclude "U.S. persons"—meaning individuals, corporations, and unincorporated associations—from (among other things) agreeing to refuse or actually refusing to do business with Israel, and impose both civil and criminal penalties for doing so.[167] That law is in effect today, and has prevented most Americans and American businesses from joining the Arab nations' boycott. Because it apparently doesn't prevent Americans from joining the BDS movement's boycotts, the legislation should be revised and expanded to the extent it would be constitutional.

---

[167] http://www.bis.doc.gov/index.php/enforcement/oac

At least one legislative proposal has been filed to strip all federal funds from academic institutions that participate in the BDS movement, but there are doubts about its First Amendment constitutionality, because it is focused on the academic boycott of Israel to which several groups and colleges have subscribed.[168]

Better legislation—to take advantage of the fact that there is no constitutional right to government contracts—could bar the government from contracting with any company, individual or academic institution that joined the BDS movement and actually refused to do business with Israel.[169] There is no apparent conflict between this approach and the First Amendment, just as there was none in the original 1976–1977 legislation. Such legislation, if passed, could be almost as powerful a tool against the BDS movement as the 1970s legislation was against the Arab boycott. Such a bill directed specifically at the BDS movement should be drafted and passed by the U.S. Congress forthwith.

For Israel, the end of the Obama presidency could mean that America will reengage in the Middle East as a positive influence.

The Future of Israeli Policy

It must become an Israeli national priority to deal with and defeat the BDS movement. Prime Minister Netanyahu mentions it in major speeches, including a March 2014 speech to AIPAC: "The BDS boycott movement is not going to stop that [Israeli tech exports], any more than the Arab movement could stop Israel from becoming a global technological power. They are going to fail."[170]

But Netanyahu is underestimating the threat of the BDS movement, perhaps gravely. This is the kind of cause that Israel can let simmer and ignore only at its peril.

The BDS movement will not just fade from view. Its funding sources—European governments, NGOs and other anti-Israel governments and organizations—have found a comfort zone in which they can reinforce each other's efforts without suffering any political—or financial—penalty.

---

168   http://freebeacon.com/house-bill-would-cut-funding-to-backers-of-israeli-boycotts/

169   "Ingalls Shipbuilding, Inc. v United States," 13 Cl. Ct. 757 (1987)

170   http://www.algemeiner.com/2014/03/04/bds-movement-will-fail-netanyahu-says-at-aipac/

In that environment they can continue their disinformation campaign against Israel indefinitely. The longer they do, the more likely Israel will find itself further isolated and less able to find reliable allies, avenues of trade, and the means of sustaining itself.

The flow of money may continue for many years, and with it the economic pressure on Israel will not abate. Israel is undoubtedly learning how best to counteract BDS, but it—like all victims of disinformation—has to do more.

Because the BDS movement is conducting an ideological war, Israel has to respond in kind. For example, many of the lessons it should apply to resist the BDS movement should have been learned in the Israel-Hizballah war in Lebanon in 2006.

In a paper prepared for the U.S.-Islamic World Forum in 2007, veteran journalist Marvin Kalb and Carol Saivetz discussed the use of the media as a weapon in asymmetrical warfare. The paper contrasts the ease with which a closed society—such as the terrorist organization of Hizballah—can create an impression of order and disciplinem while an open society—such as Israel—conveys the impression in war of disorder, chaos, and uncertainty, which can be misleading. [171]

But that is a sidebar to the main issue: the use of the media as a weapon of war wasn't new to the world, but this was the first war in which the Middle East saw instantaneous reporting of events by blog and camera. Hizballah was prepared to use this new weapon. The Israelis were not.

Information wars have been going on since Julius Caesar told the Roman Senate, "*Veni, vidi, vici.*" But it always seems to surprise a war's participants. At least since Vietnam, it boiled down to this: what you say, write, and broadcast is just as important as how well you shoot. Every aspect of a battle in every corner of the world is susceptible to biased reporting and worse.

In the 2006 war, the bias of the media was so evident that people became inured to it. As Kalb and Saivetz wrote:

---

[171] Marvin Kalb and Carol Saivetz, "The Israeli-Hezbollah War of 2006: The Media as a Weapon in Asymmetrical Conflict," Kennedy School of Government, Harvard University (February 2007); http://www.brookings.edu/~/media/events/2007/2/17islamic%20world/2007islamforum_israel%20hezb%20war.pdf

A key consequence of this new warfare is that the role of the journalist in many parts of the world has been dramatically transformed—from a quest for objectivity and fairness to an acceptance of advocacy as a tool of the craft. If once the journalist aspired to honest and detached reporting, now it has become increasingly acceptable for the journalist to be an activist player and a fiery advocate. 24/7 cable news has placed a premium on provocative chatter, not on substantive discourse. Many journalists in the Middle East, born into a culture of submissiveness to centralized authority, have always seen themselves as players and advocates, but this has not been the norm in Europe or the United States, and this change is both noteworthy and disturbing.[172]

Hizballah leader Hassan Nasrallah publicly proclaimed he would hide soldiers among civilians, but when Israel attacked the soldiers, it was they who were accused of war crimes, and it was Israel that was accused of constantly using "disproportionate" force.[173] That's because Nasrallah was entirely committed to fighting the war on television, radio, the Internet and in print, and the Israelis lagged far behind.

This is the concept of "air superiority," which is usually defined in terms of combat between aircraft but is directly applicable to the media wars. If your aircraft have air superiority, no enemy aircraft can fly in the battle space without getting shot down. In the media wars, assertions and arguments have to be shot down with facts.

Those who enjoy "air superiority" today are nations or terrorist groups who get their side of the story most quickly and effectively across to the most read, watched, and listened-to media. There is never any complete air dominance in the information war, but there can and must be a dominant effort by nations who are, like Israel, under attack by terrorists and the media that favor them.

Hizballah-sympathetic television reporters, bloggers, photographers, and reporters of almost every stripe had access to the battlefields. As we saw above, whether it was Hizballah in Lebanon or Hamas in Gaza,

---

172 Id., Kalb and Saivetz, p. 6
173 Id., pp. 7–9

these people stage-managed events and helped the media report their side of them daily, hourly and almost minute by minute. That is how they created the media narrative—the prevailing story line—through those wars.

Typically, the Arab and Palestinian newspapers were the most biased:

> *Asharq Al-Awsat* is one of the two Arabic-language newspapers published in London and then distributed throughout the Middle East. From July 13 to August 16, the paper ran 24 photographs related to the war on the front page; all but two of them showed the death and destruction in Lebanon caused by Israeli attacks. The Arab reader of this paper could have drawn only one conclusion— that Israel was guilty of converting Lebanon into a "killing field." Only once, July 31, did *Asharq Al-Awsat* show a photograph of the destruction that Hezbollah rockets were causing in Israel. This imbalance (22 to 1) could hardly be defined by a Western yardstick as "objective journalism," but it could still be explained in the context of Middle East journalism, where many Arab reporters feel a nationalistic, religious or cultural prejudice against Israel.[174]

The 2006 war—and this excellent analysis of the news coverage of it—holds three important lessons for Israel in its effort to defeat the BDS movement. They are just as applicable to the future wars Israel will have to fight with Hizballah in Lebanon and Hamas in Gaza.

The first lesson is that in the ideological war against the BDS movement's false accusations, Israel has to gain "air superiority" as best they can. They will not offset the years of BDS-sympathetic news coverage— and its effects—now or ever. But they can do a far better job on both offense and defense.

To do that, Israel needs both recruits at home and allies abroad. Israel, as the Kalb and Saivetz report shows, will always be subjected to hugely biased reporting by the Arab media. But the Arab media market is not where Israel needs to fight the BDS movement: that effort

---

[174] Id., p. 11

has to be concentrated in American, European, and even Far Eastern media, such as Japan's.

The Israelis need to have a counterweight campaign directed at major and minor media outlets in those markets designed to prove the falsity of the apartheid, racism, and war crimes charges and all the other attacks of the BDS movement. The top complaint of reporters everywhere is that they want more access to top decision-makers. They should have it. Israel, like any nation, has its secrets. But the more open it is, the fewer reporters will be skeptical of it and its actions.

Israel already embeds reporters within military units. The Israeli military, like every military since Sun Tzu, has looked askance at reporters and the media generally; but the embedding program, which Israel should probably expand, is a way to create trust on both sides of the equation. As for news coverage, there is no substitute for the truth broadcast to the world in real time. Embedded reporters can do that as no one else can.

The same approach should be taken to the next step by embedding reporters in the military and police who operate along the borders and inside the West Bank and Gaza. Demonstrating that Israel isn't a racist or apartheid state can't be explained nearly as well as it can be shown. That can't be done in a day or a week; but the longer the reporters are embedded with Israeli security forces, the better their opinion of Israel will be, and the more valuable.

The second lesson is that allies need to be looked for, and campaigned for, in unconventional places. In America, few—if any—Jewish organizations are active in opposing the BDS movement. As Herb London points out in his introduction to this book, even some of the Hillel organizations—the primary Jewish organizations on college campuses—are either antipathetic to Israel's battle against the BDS movement or sitting on the sidelines. There should be a concerted effort to gain recruits to oppose the BDS movement among the Hillel organizations and other college groups. Students need to understand how the BDS movement's goals would restrict their academic freedoms and make their education less valuable.

Another lesson is that other allies are available. In the Evangelical Christian community in America—which is composed of an enormous number of people in the Midwest and the Rocky Mountain states—there is far stronger support for Israel than among a large portion of the American Jewish community. Israel should be courting those voters and asking them to help oppose BDS. They can help change public opinion and so affect national policy.

The third lesson is in immediacy and persistence and the other aspect of "air superiority."

The April 2014 iteration of the Obama-Kerry "peace plan" failed because it proposed a return to indefensible borders, because the Palestinians won't recognize Israel as a Jewish state, and because they insist on a "right of return." The failure was made certain by the "reconciliation" planned between Hamas and Fatah. Israel needs to launch an aggressive media campaign blaming the Palestinians for the failure. That campaign should be strong enough and so widespread that it would have most major political and Israeli media figures—from the Prime Minister on down—engaged to condemn the Palestinians as the obstacle to peace they truly are.

Once this campaign begins, it should not end for months, perhaps years. There is no reason for Israelis to be reluctant to seize the media narrative and seek to control it. In air warfare, if one side can gain "air superiority," that means it has effectively barred the enemy from operating in the skies it controls. The Israelis will never gain "media superiority" in terms of controlling the media narrative globally, but they can do it in the major media markets—in America at least—and battle for it in European media.

To do that, the Israelis need to remind the media—repetitively, as many times as they'll sit still to hear it—that the Palestinians' track record is entirely consistent. At Camp David in 2000, the Palestinians could have traded land for peace but turned it down. In 2005, Ariel Sharon offered land for peace (without land swaps) and was rejected. In 2008, Ehud Olmert again offered land for peace, and his proposal wasn't even answered.

The 2014 rejection of the Obama-Kerry peace plan—again embracing the "land for peace" concept—is the fourth time in 14 years the Palestinians have refused peace. Israel's message should be loud and clear, blaming the Palestinians for their preference for war over peace. It should be stated by the Israelis persistently as the necessary answer to any of the BDS movement's fulminations.

After Obama leaves office, the new American president will need to reassess our policy toward Israel and the rest of the Middle East. If the next president is Hillary Clinton, Israel knows how it will turn out and should proceed in its own interests as it sees them. If it is anyone else, Israel needs to allow time for a new president to settle into the job before taking any major actions that directly affect America's national security. That, of course, includes military action against Iran.

If Israel believes it cannot wait any longer to strike at Iran's nuclear weapons facilities, it should give the next president at least the short time necessary to come to the conclusion that America should join in the strike. Whether or not we do so, Israel has the right—really, the obligation—to make that decision itself.

In any future war, some writers are suggesting that Israel will have to consider cooperating in U.N. and other "impartial" investigations of the fighting. They should not. There is no point in cooperating with organizations like the U.N., which have never treated Israel fairly. But they should monitor those investigations, conduct their own parallel inquiries, and be prepared to tell the truth to the world and punish any crimes committed against civilians regardless of who they may be.

As to the BDS movement, Israel should not wait for the November 2016 election. Its leaders, and their allies in America and elsewhere, should state—boldly and without doubt—that the BDS movement's case against Israel cannot withstand the light of day. Only the truth can expose the lies. They should be stated every day at every opportunity.

Obama has tried to tilt the balance toward the Palestinians. He was wrong to do so. America should not be an impartial arbiter between the parties to this conflict. There are too many in the wrong, such as the Gazans, who chose Hamas terrorists to govern them. Hamas, whose charter states that its express purpose is the destruction of Israel, is an enemy of civilization. The Palestine Authority, in the person of Mahmoud Abbas, quite evidently lacks the power to effectuate a peace and thus cannot be regarded as a representative of the Palestinian people. It is only the Israelis who, with all their imperfections, stand for freedom, just as America does.

Epilogue

IN 2003, I WAS ESCORTED through the Israeli military compound in Gaza by a young Israeli officer from Ethiopia. As we were walking, he told me something about his personal odyssey.

Eighteen years before, an uncle had walked a thousand miles from Sudan to Ethiopia to deliver a toddler to an Israeli mission called Operation Rescue. The toddler's parents wanted to remove the child from a hostile environment and send him to a place where he would be welcomed, educated, and comforted.

The boy became a man rooted in the soil of the Jewish state. He welcomed the opportunity to join the military on his 18th birthday and by dint of achievement rose through the ranks to become an officer.

He had one dream, and that was to bring his parents to Israel, parents he knew only through correspondence and photographs. In 2001, that dream was realized. His parents joined him in Tel Aviv. It was a joyous occasion filled with tears and stories.

Two weeks after his arrival, the father was hit by a truck and killed as he crossed an avenue against the light. All the joy of arrival turned into despair. Upon learning of this death, government officials sent the young man a letter indicating that since he now had responsibility for the support of his mother, military service was no longer required.

The officer pulled a letter out of his pocket and read it to me. It was his reply to the authorities: "I will find a way to care for the mother I am only now starting to know, but do not ask me to give up the mother I know and love, i.e. the Israeli Defense Force, the mates in my unit, the nation I am honored to serve."

He spoke with remarkable passion and conviction as this letter was read. As I listened, the words "Israeli apartheid" entered my consciousness. South African apartheid was based on racial separation. Here in Israel I found the exact opposite condition, a black man in a nation that has him in its bosom and to whom he has given his love and trust. He is the face of modern Israel: proud, strong, patriotic, and multiracial.

It is instructive that at a paratrooper induction I attended, volunteers (paratroopers are not draftees) receive a bible and a rifle at a ceremony filled with emotion. What is most interesting is that about a third I observed on my last trip to Israel were black men, men who are devoted to their nation and its survival.

It is not only Arabs that live and thrive side by side with Jews, but Ethiopians and Africans and Christians of every denomination. Zionism is inclusive, as any objective observer of Israeli society knows. Yet this reality is conspicuously absent from the BDS narrative.

What, then, can be done? First, it pays to tell the truth again and again, at least as often as the lies. Social media can be an ally in what has been described as a goal of "air superiority." Let every Arab child and teenager receive tweets about the reality of Israeli life. Let Arab girls wonder why they are not afforded the same opportunities as Israeli girls.

Second, legislation should be promoted at the U.S. state and federal level that denies public funds for support of any aspect of BDS. This would not be a First Amendment dodge, but rather an admonition that the spreading of lies, hate, and slander should not be financed by taxpayer money.

Third, it is important for those who defend Israeli positions to track the activities of the BDS faithful and wherever and whenever possible challenge their positions. This isn't easy, nor is it predictable. Yet it is an essential element in defeating scurrilous claims that often go unanswered.

Lastly, it is our belief, based on common sense and empirical evidence, that the current round of peace negotiations was bound to fail. Israel is not about to commit suicide to satisfy an Obama administration that eagerly wants a deal, and the PLO will never relinquish its desire for "the right of return" and the nonrecognition of a Jewish state. Since stalemate is the likely outcome, supporters of Israel should use the occasion to point out which party is truly intransigent. The BDS movement will fail when it is clear that peace is not at hand because of PLO obduracy.

In fact, it is imperative that the public affairs organs of Israel reiterate what most sensible people know. If Israel unilaterally disarms, the nation will be destroyed. If the reverse were to occur—i.e., the Arab states disarm—peace would be at hand.

When war clouds were on the horizon in 1937, George Orwell said, "The first duty of intelligent men is the restatement of the obvious." This is as true today as it was then. Israel is an open, multiethnic, and multiracial democracy that sits proudly as a bulwark against slavish and totalitarian states in its neighborhood. This point must be made every day and on every occasion. It is the very issue BDS glosses over or chooses to ignore, and it is the central issue in the ideational war confronting the Middle East and even within the professoriate at home.

HERBERT LONDON

Acknowledgements

THE AUTHORS WISH TO THANK Adam Bellow, David Bernstein, and the rest of the team at Liberty Island Media for their assistance in producing this book. We also wish to thank Rabbi Binyamin Sendler and General Ion Pacepa for allowing us to use at least a small part of their vast stores of wisdom and Bryan Griffin for his superb research.

Appendix

NGO	Primary Funder(s)	Funding Amount	Central Involvement
Addameer	Sweden	€207,000 (2009)	Signatory to 2005 BDS call (http://www.bdsmovement.net/)
	NDC*	$250,000	
Al Haq	Netherlands	$461,201(2008)	BDS is part of mission statement
	Diakonia	$204,134 (2008)	
	NDC*	$150,000	
	Norway, Ireland	n/a	
Al Mezan	Sweden	€105,000 (2007–9)	Signatory to 2005 BDS call (http://www.bdsmovement.net/)
	NDC*	$500,000	
	Norway, EU	n/a	
Alternative Information Center	Ireland, Sweden (via Diakonia), Catalan gov't	n/a	"Yes to Boycott, Divestment and Sanctions (BDS) Against Israel"
Alternatives (Montreal)	Canada	$C2 million (2008–10; halted?)	Signatory to 2005 BDS call (http://www.bdsmovement.net/)
Applied Research Institute Jerusalem (PA)	EU	€374,174 (2009–11)	Signatory to 2005 BDS call (http://www.bdsmovement.net/)
	Spain	€98,347 (2009)	
	Switzerland	n/a	
Badil (PA)	NDC*	$100,000	Leader of BDS movement
Christian Aid	U.K., Ireland, EU	combined €22 million (2007–8)	"Partner supporting" calling for BDS and "pursuing parastata Zionist orgs"
Coalition of Women for Peace	EU	€247,954 (2005–7)	Runs "Who profits?" website, which is central in the Norwegian BDS campaign
	NIF	$285,509 (2006–8)	
Defence of Children International – Palestine Section	Sweden	€316,000 (2009[1])	Signatory to 2005 BDS call (http://www.bdsmovement.net/)
	NDC*	$450,000	
Diakonia	Sweden	$42.7 million (2008)	Advocates for divestment strategy against Israel; lobbies against EU-Israel upgrade
	EU	n/a	

NGO	Primary Funder(s)	Funding Amount	Central Involvement
Human Rights Watch	Soros' Open Society Institute	$2,353,895(2007–8)	Supported Caterpillar boycott; called for cuts in U.S. foreign aid to Israel
	Ford Foundation	$445,000 (2009–11)	
	Netherlands via Oxfam-NOVIB	$987,818 (2007–8)	
Israel Committee Against House Demolitions (ICAHD)	Spain	€105,000 (2009)	Leader in BDS activism
	NDC*	$80,000	
KAIROS	Canada. Funding was recently halted.	$1,575,966 (2008)	Main supporter of church divestment campaign
Machsom Watch	EU	€251,650 (2007–10)	Norwegian Pension Fund divestment campaign
	NIF	$165,198 (2006–8)	
Miftah	EU	$100,531(2008)	Signatory to 2005 BDS call (http://www.bdsmovement.net/)
	Denmark	$101,767 (2008)	
	Norway	$129,870 (2008)	
Mossawa	NIF	$517,642 (2006–8)	Norwegian Pension Fund divestment campaign
	EU	€298,660(2006–8)	
	U.K.	n/a	
Norwegian Association of NGOs for Palestine (incl. Norwegian People's Aid)	Norway	€57,000 (2008)	Coordinates Norwegian Boycott Israel Campaign
	USA	€8,000 (2008)	
	Sweden, Netherlands	n/a	
Palestinian NGO Network (PNGO)	NDC*	$130,000	Leader of BDS movement
	Received France's Human Rights Prize		
Sabeel	Sweden	€76,000 (2006–8)	Leader of global church divestment movement
Trocaire	Ireland	€23,499,837 (2008)	Supports BDS movement; lobbies against EU-Israel upgrade; calls for review of arms export licenses
	UK	€640,682 (2008)	
	EU	€1,698,692 (2008)	
War on Want	UK	€256,000 (2008)	Advocates for sanctions, including arms boycott
	Ireland	€77,000 (2008)	
	EU	€266,000 (2008)	

(SOURCE: NGO MONITOR)

*The NDC mechanism is funded by Switzerland, Sweden, Denmark, and Netherlands; 2008–2009

Made in the USA
Charleston, SC
04 September 2014